PRAISE FOR SUE FREDERICK'S WORK

"This book is a treasure for anyone wishing to understand how to be fully functional in the world while at the same time immersed in spiritual growth and learning. The writing is a treat in itself – elegant and enchanting. Sue's words drew me in to the quiet place inside. This book is a precious gem of love, compassion, forgiveness and transcendence."
— Faith Stone, author of *Drawing Buddhas and Bodhisattvas;*
and *The Kitchen Goddess*

"I enjoyed this book in a profound way; it's a spiritual adventure so close to mine."
— Syntysche Groverland, Minister,
Unity of Boulder

"One of the most delicious memoirs to have appeared on bookshelves in many years. Its lyrical passages read like songs."
— Devin Patrick Hughes, Music Director,
Boulder Symphony

"Sue has written an honest homage to love: love of men, love of God, love of gurus. She morphs romance and worship in her search for a partner and for life's meaning, creating a new genre, the romantic spiritual memoir."
— Donna M.Gershten, award-winning author of
Kissing the Virgin's Mouth

ISBN: 978-0-9762393-4-5
Library of Congress Control Number: 2017908779

WATER OAK

THE HAPPINESS OF LONGING
A Memoir

SUE FREDERICK

This book is for Sarah.

Contents

PART ONE:
THE FIRE

You live for the way the Water Oak loves you and you love it; so it's no surprise when during the worst of the storm; in the thick of the 30 foot waves, your enormous tree uproots itself to save you all; uses its branches to lift your homes and families towards heaven, into heaven, until the waves recede and the tree carries you safely down to earth, to the devastated land; placing your two homes exactly back on their concrete foundations, undamaged, and crushing Miss Camille the same way Dorothy's home once crushed the wicked witch of the east.

Then everything is perfect. Forever. Paul's ashes never swim in the tiny lake and you never leave the south or disappoint your family and no one ever dies or breaks your heart – and your father, well your father....

But then all of this wouldn't have happened and you'd probably still be a lost girl living in the south without your religion.

So maybe you were loved so much, cherished really, that you were sent on the road to Oz because you needed to go. And it was Miss Camille who loved you enough to send you there; so that much later you'd realize you'd always been wearing the ruby slippers.

Perhaps Miss Camille was your greatest spiritual teacher as she blew her 200-mile-per-hour winds, aimed them directly at your Long Beach; she destroyed you. All of you. Like an angry Durga; like the wrathful Kali.

And all the losses that came afterwards were nothing compared to standing on those piles of broken and twisted Water

Oak branches to find your Grandpa's rusted wrench in the rubble. Nothing ever stood up to that loss. For anyone.

And when you write about your husband dying young or Crissie your Crissie or all the wrong men you chose to love and the grief you fought so hard to lift, you realize that it all began with Long Beach and your surprise visit from Miss Camille in 1969.

This tale of Christopher leaving is nothing compared to those other things but you tell it because it's the way we are, us people, us women, the way we keep picking up the pieces and carrying on until one day another loss, maybe an unimportant one such as a suitcase disappearing while you're traveling or another man walking out your door, and this new rather insignificant loss jumps on top of your pile of grievances, stands on your broken foundation; and suddenly you come undone.

And becoming undone is the one true thing you really need to do.

So you thank your Miss Camille. Your Durga. Your devastation.

And you begin your story here...

I

The Midnight Visit

December 1990: Mazatlan Mexico

It's 2 am on a warm night in Mazatlan when a sandy-haired man wearing khaki shorts and a white t-shirt jumps over our balcony railing and comes round the bed. He's barefoot. The swiftness of his leap onto our railing is what draws my attention and pulls me from my dreams.

It's a beautiful room, moonlit and airy, with a high ceiling and a breeze from the Sea of Cortez fluttering through as I lay watching the stranger use his strong, tanned arms to balance briefly on the railing, land firmly on the floor, and walk directly to me - where I lay cuddled and afraid next to Christopher.

At first I'm paralyzed, unable to move, and as he comes closer I scream and struggle to sit up, kicking and punching to push him away. But soon enough I understand, and as Christopher awakes and reaches for his bedside lamp it's clear, no one stands beside the bed.

There's a moment of stunned silence, as we both survey the empty room, then Christopher dives towards me, wrapping his arms around me. "What did you see?" His tone is urgent, confused. "What is it?"

"A man was here beside the bed. Didn't you see him? He jumped over the balcony. His feet made noise hitting the floor. He was real." I pull away from Christopher and stand up, breathless and heart pounding. "Help me search the room."

Christopher gets up, nervously running his hand through his tousled blonde hair, blinking his eyes to clear the sleep, moving carefully through the room, holding a book in one hand as a weapon, checking under the bed, in the closets and bathroom. I pace beside him anxiously, then move to the balcony to look down at the sea, at the white-foamed waves crashing on the small rocky stretch of sand far beneath our balcony.

We're five floors up. How could that man have jumped from mid-air to land on our balcony?

"Tell me exactly what you saw, Sue," says Christopher, voice low and sweet, standing beside me on the balcony. He knows me well and has already begun to realize that this is one of my ghosts, yet the lingering energy of the event has shaken him. He looks pale and there are glimmering beads of sweat dotting his forehead. He guides me to the bed. "Look at me, Sue. Take a deep breath. There's no one in the room."

"I know," I whisper exhaling deeply, feeling incredulous and shaken. "He was so real."

"Who was he? What did he want?" whispers Christopher taking my hand, sitting on the bed beside me.

I describe the man, how he leapt over the railing so purposefully, how deliberately he walked around the bed, but not like he wanted to hurt me, instead like he wanted to tell me something.

Christopher shivers, "I can still feel him in the room." Almost to distract himself, he gets up, shuts the glass doors to the balcony and double-checks the bolt on the door to the hallway, leaving all the lights on as he sits back down on the bed.

Nestling next to me under the sheets he says, "I believe you saw someone. I have no doubt. I can feel it. His energy is still here. But why would a spirit want to bother you? Or us?"

I don't answer. I don't know. Christopher becomes quiet. After awhile he says slowly, "There are people who don't want us here... together," holding me very tightly. "It could be the spirit of someone trying to hurt us."

Wrapping his legs around mine and burying his face in my hair, he whispers, "I love you so much."

In the ensuing troubled silence, I feel his mind processing a series of instant brain synapses, deftly navigating his famous mercurial shift, as sudden as the sound of the strange man landing on the balcony. In one instant, Christopher has set a new course. He will leave me. Soon.

This is the price he pays for his brilliance, his quick wittedness, the nimble mind that can move lithely from one extraordinary business idea to a completely opposing point of view; the intelligence that fuels his role as president of a large chain of natural foods stores, a multi-million dollar company that doubles and triples its growth at every turn.

Yet he carries this nimble cleverness into his personal life where it can make him unrecognizable to those who love him; fluidly shifting allegiances, betraying friendships and falling in love with strangers. He's ruled by the wind, a sail without mooring, fleeting, brief and glorious, anchorless and thrilling.

I will love you forever. I will leave you tomorrow.

Those of us who love Christopher, and there are many - including a wife and two children he recently separated from - find ourselves doubled over and breathless from his sudden deviations, searching for solid ground, reaching for the wind as he disappears.

I usually try to wait it out, allowing him to change direction again, sensing that his sweetness, his openhearted love is a gift worth my patience.

He's something to behold, face shaped like a cherub with soft generous rosy lips and the curly golden hair of a Greek God, smooth fair skin, eyes blue and vivid. From the moment we first spoke on a Colorado Mountaintop during a ski trip one year earlier, our alchemy had been sparked, our paths intertwined, our recognition startling and unavoidably course changing.

He saw my sensitivity and embraced it; when a spirit roused me in the night or my intuition changed our plans, he was curious and patient. He wanted to hear every story I had to tell and savor every inch of my body. I was delighted, utterly disarmed and unable to say no.

We knew each other's wounds. My tale of grief, of a dying husband ten years earlier, had not scared him, but rather pulled him magnetically towards me because of his own unquenchable thirst for wisdom, for depth, for something he saw hidden inside of me; a strength and truth he was trying to grasp for himself, a pull to something deeper, both terrifying and seductive.

His childhood memories were of a distant alcoholic mother and a philandering physician father whom he adored. His love for women was fueled by his need for a mother's love and he understood that. And I had seen my beloved New Orleans father in Christopher since the moment we met, but it was more. Losing my husband to cancer had turned me upside down, tilted my soul off kilter. Longing for Christopher, an impossible man, was as familiar as grieving the departed.

As the endless Mazatlan night, with waves pounding relentlessly, rolls to its inevitable conclusion, I know I've lost Christopher. For good.

Our wild and fearless love is nothing to leave a family for, to break the hearts of innocent babes or a loyal wife. "We" have become an unsolvable dilemma, and the ghost jumping over the railing has been his heavenly messenger, a spirit sent to hurt me. Or so he believes.

And looking back, I see the wisdom of the sandy haired man invading our private domain, someone sent from another realm to shake me loose of something, to wake me up, to be my divine reveal. But this is not how I saw it that tormented evening, sudden winds whipping up the sea below us, Christopher's long legs wrapped tightly around mine, neither of us able to sleep.

Though we stay in Mazatlan for the full week of our vacation, crying as we make love, kissing every crevice, savoring each moment, knowing each other's thoughts, Christopher is already moving back home with his family.

So later in my Colorado apartment when he says with tears in his eyes: "I'm going home. I have to," there's nothing left in me to fight it. I stand empty in front of him, my arms reaching out as he pulls away, bones turning to chalk.

I can't live without you, he had said. But now he would. And he would be fine.

As Christopher packs his things, I fade, withdraw; my spirit slips up out the top of my head, floating above us.

He searches my apartment to be sure he hasn't left anything and walks out the door with his soft blue shirt taking his thick scent, sucking the air from the room, and his golden tussled hair taking the light.

This is all too familiar, too old, I realize, collapsing on the floor. There's so much to learn in this moment of heartbreak, a part of me understands. But I can't see the lesson, can't find my way through the pain.

Alone I sit in silence until the emptiness of the air becomes deafening, a loud hum, and I run to the door, swing it open and slump in the doorway howling like a feral cat, dangerous and desperate. My inner voice demanding, "What is wrong with me?"

I'm jinky-janked and broken; pitiful and sorry; I know nothing and everything; and this is all my doing because all I ever had to say was "no" - don't fly in to see me; no, don't call; don't put your hand there, your mouth here, your scent there; and instead I wanted everything, everything he could offer, until I wanted too much and that became a poison; and now I must puke it all up, drain it from my veins, purge myself of longing for what I'll never have; and that is the sorriest thing a person can be; and here I sit hungry and tired in an empty room hoping the world will feed me.

How have I fallen so far from grace? What was the choice I made but shouldn't have; should've made but didn't? How has my endless longing delivered me here broken and sorry, twisted and rejected, when once I was a stellar girl, a girl of promise and hope; award winning in this and that, the beauty of youth on my side, more men than I could choose; and now I've become that thing, the one people pity; oh her husband died of cancer; oh her boyfriend left her; oh she's unlucky in love; how did I land here when I was once there - on the road to salvation, skipping down the yellow brick path to Oz, my white picket fence just on the horizon so close, so close, could almost touch it, almost see my children standing by the gate; and I would have everything – the career, the man, the family - all of it flawless, stainless; transcendent; but now I find myself alone and starving.

Who sees ghosts in their hotel room during a luxurious beach vacation? Who does that and ruins things, disappoints men that way; has weird and wiry hair that must be noisily blow-dried to sleek perfection as soon as it's wet, before going out for the day, before leaving the bathroom; or suddenly they become of a different ethnicity entirely from what was expected; from who entered the bathroom.

Who exhibits such a vast difference between their flawed olive skinned pitifulness upon wakening to the glossy image once groomed; the sleek blonde haired beauty who has learned so well to hide her flaws, her un-acceptables; and yet rising in the hotel room naked, too thin, too wiry haired, too big nosed is something her mother always warned her of – the disturbing French Creole blood mixed with slave blood that is never what a perfect blue-eyed prince is seeking.

Yes I relentlessly seek the perfect blue-eyed prince even though none of them love me; or at least none of them can stay; and why was my mother's jangled up family all olive-skinned and dark eyed while my father came from the light; entered a room with blue eyes that were clearly a direct channel from God; eyes that carried love into a lonely room; his fair skinned pale eyed beauty sacrificed at the family altar for our happiness.

This is an unfair set up dear God; you've stacked the odds too high against me; bet too strongly on my losses; from where you sit in heaven my chosen lifetime must have seemed ridiculous to you and yet you let me slide down into it; through my mother's dark fear and out into a world where blue eyed men, princes of the sea, would mean everything and I would pursue them wildly yet they would never ever love me truly; never deem me worthy; especially when my ghostly dreams disturbed us in the night or I had feelings, God forbid feelings, in a world of pale skinned men with brilliant minds who carried their hearts so deeply buried.

Does it all come down to this? Was my mother right after all? Christopher's wife must've been easier wasn't she? Wash and wear, wrinkle-free; while I require care and special handling; too many things from my past bubbling up to haunt; too many gag reflexes from caring for dying husbands; too many nightmares screaming me out of bed in the night; too much time spent in the bathroom blow-drying and painting over imperfections.

What happened to my God; to the Jesus I grew up praying to and the Mother Mary I saw in my dreams as a child; where are the saints and angels who once comforted me; the yoga poses and meditations all designed to enlighten; no one pursues all of that so vigorously and still ends up pitiful and lonely on a cold floor in a broken room in a broken house inside a broken life when they are only just nearly 40 and have tried everything, tried so hard to be good and true, determined, hopeful, hard working and strong; and none of that has mattered, not one iota of it has mattered; or Christopher would have stayed; and Paul would have survived cancer; and my mother, my damaged mother, would have loved me anyway.

I am the muddy Mississippi River swirling dark and angry, drowning anyone who tries to enter; I'm dizzy and dangerous; floating past all of you blue-eyed and perfect, waving and toasting from the shore – all of you sainted, saved; married, mothered, loved and un-alone.

I am a soulless howler. I am a hungry ghost. Be wary of me. What I have may be catching; my lovers seem to think it's so.

2

ANOTHER DAY AT NEW TIMES

February 1991: Boulder Colorado

"Sue, we need to talk," says Margaret, my boss at the publishing company where I work, one hand brushing luxurious dark hair back from her face, rounded lips turned flat into a line of worry. "The cover you chose for the August issue. It's just not right," searching my eyes intently. "I don't like the photo, there's something off about it."

My passionate and stormy friendship with Margaret had begun the day our CEO, Gordon, hired her and proudly called us into his office to meet our new sales director. She entered the room in a flurry of black cashmere and silk, voluptuous and intoxicating, fresh from New York and a sales career at HBO.

She was fearless and carefree, throwing her head back to laugh heartily when she flubbed a name during introductions. She had east coast, Kenyon-educated confidence, bred from a family of alcoholic geniuses, her father the original "Mad Man" who'd created numerous iconic campaigns of the 50s, 60s and 70s. Her mother was the glamorous Jackie Kennedy of a small town in Connecticut, the wealthiest town in America.

I would later learn that Margaret's childhood was fraught with vodka-fueled parental rages, family evenings turned abusive, and a clamoring and desperate brood of siblings clawing over one another to be deemed the wittiest and win dad's rare approval.

Margaret had eventually broken free from her powerful family to arrive out west in Boulder, looking for a new start, a healthier way to live, when she stumbled upon my magazine with its articles on healthy lifestyle, herbs, vitamins and preventative nutrition. "I've got to meet these people," she had said to a stranger in a bar who turned out to be a friend of Gordon's. Introductions were made, meetings set up and within weeks she was our new publishing executive and my new boss.

From the moment we met I loved her - not for her charming personality or brilliant mind. I loved her vulnerability. In spite of her cool confident exterior, her breathless beauty, I saw her pain and she saw mine; life had taught us both that surfaces mostly lie and that what lingers beneath is the treasure worth finding.

We had understood from that first meeting that all the richness of a true timeless friendship lived between us and beyond us – far outside of our roles as editor and sales executive and that our love would entangle us in each other's lives forever. Shaking hands in Gordon's office that day, we both saw it unfolding, though no one spoke it. We couldn't wait to begin.

It began just days later during a business trip. We were assigned to room together at the Anaheim Marriott during our company's twice-annual week-long Natural Products Expo – a ridiculously huge and stressful convention for the natural products industry that Gordon had launched years ago and had become our company's largest revenue source.

Retailers and manufacturers from around the world flocked to Anaheim to rent our booths, sell their products, attend our seminars and parties, and grow their businesses. The event poured buckets of money into New Times' coffers. And for the first several years, including the year Margaret joined New Times, our company of around 30 employees ran the event 24/7 without hiring outside help.

My first Expo was a baptism of fire, learning quickly that attendance at every event was mandatory and assistance with everything from arranging food for a dance party to hanging banners in the hall was required. Staff members were fired on the spot for not showing up to an event on time or failing to put in their hours of networking. You either drank the New Times Cool Aid or were kicked off the bus.

I found the pressure heady and intoxicating; I loved getting to know brilliant natural health doctors, herbalists, homeopaths and authors and convincing them to travel without pay to teach a seminar for the industry.

They became my friends; brilliant, quirky herbalists who chewed on raw ginger, homeopathic doctors who taught the quantum physics of healing, and tofu makers who went overnight from selling their wares from the back of a truck to signing million dollar business deals.

It was all a non-stop, rock-festival orgy of grown up hippies who were making a living doing what they loved. I fit right into this crowd of offbeat, alternative-seeking, children of the 60s. And I took my expo duties as serious as a heart-attack, – up at 5 am to moderate the herbal seminars and not back to my room until well after midnight - for seven days straight.

Until I met Margaret.

As we unpacked that first night in Anaheim, dividing dresser drawers, choosing sides of the closet, we already felt like an old married couple negotiating wake up times, bathroom counter space and room for our abundant shoes.

As soon as we settled in, I told Margaret we needed to run and catch the staff bus headed to the event center so we could set up the booth for the next day's events. She waved her hand in the air and said, "That's ridiculous," laughing breathlessly. "We're here to sell the magazine, to look successful and worldly, not exhausted and terrified. There are plenty of people around to set up that booth."

"But Gordon won't be happy about that," I stammered. "You don't understand how..."

"We will arrive late," she announced, hands on her hips, tossing her hair back and straightening her shoulders, looking like a dark-haired Marilyn Monroe. "We'll say we're impossibly busy with important meetings, selling ads, you know, the money stuff." Smiling warmly at me, "Honey relax. We need a luxurious room service dinner and a quiet night. We're going to sell the shit out of our magazine this week. Trust me. Gordon won't be firing anybody after we weave our magic."

"Cinda (our CFO) doesn't allow room service," I offered hesitantly. "We have a travel budget."

But Margaret was already on the phone ordering lobster tails, Caesar salad, a bottle of wine and chocolate mousse for dessert. I was beside myself with happiness, giggling as they wheeled it in, like a starving child waking up from a famine. Margaret was over-the-top excess, business-confident, deeply wounded and hilariously brilliant. I'd met a soul mate, a life-long friend. We never left our room that night, gleefully shirking our expo duties.

Digging into her lobster, Margaret asked me to share my intuitive impressions of everyone we worked with at New Times. She was a firm believer in intuition and we'd already shared ghost stories, dream visitations, astrology and numerology readings. When I'd done her numbers and explained that she'd come in on the path of the visionary, to be a leader of new thought, her eyes had gotten huge: "Wow! That explains so much," and then laughing, "and why I have so much trouble with men. And you know what honey? I truly WAS my father's favorite."

Over wine and chocolate mousse we disintegrated into giggles over New Times' glaring dysfunctions: "Does Cinda really steal toilet paper from public bathrooms to stock our offices?" "Yes, yes," howling with laughter, spitting chocolate mousse across the table. "And why does Jane's lace slip ALWAYS show beneath her dress every frickin day – the seductress of New Times! She should win an award!" Margaret standing up to place the crown on Jane's imaginary head then falling over with laughter.

Tears in our eyes, gut-splitting giggles, tripping over shoes running to the bathroom to pee. "Let's toast to Gordon's fucking genius - hiring mostly women to run his company, all of us overachieving bitches desperate for love," glasses clinking. "Here, Here to Gordon!"

"Did I tell you that people in the industry call us Gordon's Angels?"

"Of course they do. And they're right," holding her glass up high. "But WE will live at the top of the New Times food chain, you and I, a fearless and BEAUTIFUL team of Angels," howling again when she nearly slid off the chair from laughing, "We'll rise to the top my dear! I know this game. Trust me."

And so we did; working seamlessly from that first business trip, signing on dozens of new advertisers and convincing countless retailers to carry our magazine. Within twelve months we'd fabulously re-designed and updated our magazine on a shoestring budget, doubled ad sales and tripled circulation. We knew how to use our assets (her breathless charm and savvy business mind) alongside my rich knowledge of natural health and how to craft a magazine for reader loyalty.

"Does anyone ever say no to you two?" asked Jerome, the owner of a huge supplement company as he signed a yearlong advertising contract with us.

"Not really," answered Margaret, smiling broadly at him, pale skin glowing, tossing her thick dark hair from her face, chin raised, "So don't even think about it Jerome."

We played together as well as we worked: climbing every peak along the foothills of Boulder; swapping childhood stories as we sat atop Mt. Sanitas overlooking the snow covered continental divide. "My father has never gone a day without vodka. It's a miracle he's alive," she'd say leaning back against a warm rock, the sunlight turning her hair to black silk.

"Well, my mother went to bed with pills prescribed by her doctor for 'nervousness' when I was in eighth grade. She didn't get up until I graduated high school. I had three younger siblings to take care of."

"Wicked," she'd say. "Just wicked. How did we survive?"

We loved going to the opera and spent summer evenings driving the long curvy highways from Boulder to Central City or to Denver for La Boheme, Aida, and again for Le Nozze di Figaro and Don Giovanni. We shared the gloomy details of our romances; her latest fling with a younger man, my lingering grief over my husband Paul's death and my disturbing, addictive relationship with Christopher. We were bonded through a vague spiritual hunger for meaning, and both in need of deep inner tweaking though we could not see it yet.

In our first year of friendship, in the flush of our early business success, we had convinced each other that we were doing enough good in the world by creating a magazine that helped people live healthier lives.

But it was a fragile house of cards and would soon come tumbling down. Christopher's exit was the first card in my house to fall.

Leaning on the wall of page proofs outside my office door, studying me, Margaret sighs, "Let's talk honey," her voice low and sweet. "I know we can agree on an alternative cover. Do you have time right now?" Arms crossed, clearly not going anywhere until I say yes.

We've tangled before. I'm certainly ripe for a fight today. She senses my simmering anger and her face softens. "Let's go into your office." She pushes me gently inside.

"It's my job to choose the cover, Margaret," I say hotly, aware that my eyes have filled with tears, willing them not to spill, moving away from her and standing behind my desk, arms crossed.

Inside I feel cold and migraine-y and like I might puke. It takes so much effort to hide my grief, tightly bound as a noose around my throat. There will be no sympathy for me when word gets out about Christopher.

Everyone who knew Christopher had warned me. Gordon had introduced me to Christopher a year earlier as we all piled into a chairlift in Breckenridge. "Sue, this is someone you should know," patting Christopher on the back. "You're both from New Orleans and Christopher is the president of the largest chain of natural foods stores. And" voice getting sweeter, softer, "Sue is the editor of Delicious Magazine."

"I know who Sue is," said Christopher taking my ski-gloved hand and not letting go. "I've wanted to meet you for awhile," he said holding my gaze with his pale and radiant eyes."

Weeks later Gordon saw me at a restaurant having dinner with Christopher. Gordon had dropped into my office the next morning, closed the door and sat down. "He'll hurt you," he said flatly.

Then softening: "I love you Sue, you know I do. You're like a sister to me. And I know what you've been through with your husband. But Christopher." He shook his head. "Christopher was my best friend once. I've known him a long time, and he hurt me badly - in a business deal - like no one has ever hurt me. He'll hurt you too. He can't be trusted and he'll never really leave his family," He stared across the desk at me, eyes clear and sharp.

"But they've already separated, Gordon," I replied steadily. "He has his own apartment. He says he loves me."

"I'm sure he does. But it doesn't matter. He's done this before." Gordon gazed out the window thoughtfully, perhaps deciding which of Christopher's transgressions he should share with me, then changing his mind, shaking his head and standing up. "You'll get hurt here." His voice cool, then suddenly leaning over my desk, "You're doing a great job with the magazine and I don't want Christopher to hurt you. I need you here. AND you deserve someone better."

"I understand what you're saying, Gordon. But I'm in this. Over my head," I answered nervously, shifting in my chair, foot kicking.

He nodded and whispered, "Be careful," then left my office, closing the door with one last unreadable glance towards me.

Gordon was dark-haired and square-jawed, with sharp blue eyes and shrewd features. I would have been attracted to him except that he felt like my brother from the first day we met. He had a kind of harsh beauty that intimidated, especially when he ran meetings; abruptly asking questions, demanding answers, negotiating impossible deals, his brilliance sucking the air from the room, leaving everyone speechless and frantic.

But when he smiled his boyish grin, jet black Elvis Presley hair sweeping across his forehead, or giggling like a child at crude jokes, he revealed his true self – a clever prankster who'd learned the art of money making while selling drugs to finance his college education. He'd grown up in a harsh southern family with little money or comfort, and an unforgiving Christian father. He'd been determined to never be poor again, and when he realized his propensity for a business deal, even an illegal one, he dropped out of college to become a rule-breaking, Fortune-500 entrepreneur who was often invited to speak at Harvard's business school.

On the day he'd hired me, years before, when he'd moved the company to Boulder, his ivy-league-educated, porcelain-skinned first wife had sat beside me on the interview couch, reading through my portfolio of published articles, asking thoughtful questions, while Gordon paced hurriedly through the room, making urgent business calls and casting cool glances my way – stopping only briefly to ask where I was from.

When I replied, "New Orleans and Mobile," his face cracked into an impish grin and he put his phone down. "I'm from Arkansas," he announced proudly, hands digging into his jean pockets. "Tell me where you lived in Mobile."

As we exchanged southern stories, he suddenly said, "You'd make a great editor for the magazine," and abruptly left the room while his soft-spoken wife carefully explained that they were interviewing many others and I might get a phone call later in the week, "but there were so many applicants still to interview."

The phone call came from Gordon the next day with a salary offer I couldn't refuse, and hardly a moment to get a word in except to ask, "When do I start?"

We'd become fast friends over the years, our friendship built on honesty and humor. He pushed me hard to make the magazine better, even though he couldn't explain what better looked liked on my shoestring budget, with only one freelance writer to help me. He took me to countless meetings in California, New York, Texas, Utah so I would get to know the "important" industry leaders and hear their feedback on the magazine.

He was wicked smart, fierce and to the point, until something made him laugh. Then he became a giggling mischievous southern boy. Not many people saw the little boy side of him and many New Times employees considered him cruel and even crazy.

I loved it when he'd enter my office in a thrill, eyes wide and filled with light: "There's a book you HAVE to read. I was up all night reading this," tossing it on my desk. "You'll LOVE this writer!"

Or when we met after a day of skiing and all he wanted to know was whom had I met on the chairlift and what had they said that was interesting, and of course, what did they do for a living.

After a day of meetings, he wanted to know who I thought was the smartest person in the room and why. I learned to observe things more deeply because of him, preparing myself for what he would ask me later.

He broke all the rules of business; famously walking through our offices and firing employees on the spot for "bad energy." Yet the office always felt better, happier when that person was gone. "If someone isn't right for the job, Sue, fire them. You're doing them a favor in the long run. And there's always someone better waiting in the wings."

And dammit he seemed to be right about that.

Over time, he opened himself to me, looking for an insightful friend as his marriage disintegrated, ripping the company in two with his cruel divorce. His wife, brilliant and shrewd as he was, took their only child back home to Pennsylvania, threatening to take the company down with her exit. He retaliated by firing everyone she'd hired. I felt lucky to be standing when the dust from his personal crisis had cleared.

After his divorce, he became fascinated with New Age ideas, bringing me books by Marianne Williamson and Deepak Chopra, long before the world had discovered them, inviting shamans and senators to drop by our offices and share their stories. We had lively discussions about intuition and pre-cognitive dreams; he respected my gifts in those realms and was beginning to realize his own. He'd become a painter suddenly, dreaming of an image one night and waking to paint it, a golden bird, stunning and wild.

But the memory of Gordon's stern warning about Christopher haunted me in the days and weeks following our break-up. I'd been ashamed to admit to Gordon that it was over. Or to anyone.

And as Margaret stood in front of me in my office that day, arms crossed, I felt found out. "Sue, what's wrong with you?" she demanded, half knowing the answer. "You've been fighting with everyone. I've heard complaints from your staff. Gordon is worried. We're all worried."

"I'm fine," I say looking down, unable to keep the tears from running down my cheeks.

"Oh honey," she sighs, coming around the desk to hug me. "Oh honey. It's Christopher, isn't it?"

"I'm sorry," pulling away to look at me, holding me by the shoulders. "But we sorta knew this would happen. Didn't we?" Hands around my waist, "You're so tiny. Are you eating? Can I take you to dinner? Or at least for dessert?" laughing breathlessly, her eyes dark and kind against her magnificent pale skin.

"Now?" I ask barely cracking a smile.

"I'll get my purse," she announces happily. "We'll meet outside," giggling as she tiptoes towards the door. "We have to be sneaky," and laughing again she swings the door open and disappears.

We give excuses of a meeting somewhere and soon we're walking fast down the sidewalk, heels clicking on the concrete, heading towards the downtown Boulder mall.

"We want to see the dessert menu," announces Margaret to the waitress as soon as we sit down at our favorite café.

With the mid-afternoon sun pouring through the large glass windows, we devour two orders of "Death by Chocolate" and two thick and creamy cappuccinos until we feel mostly sick and I've told her the story of Christopher leaving. She listens quietly, fascinated by the ghost coming into the room in Mazatlan.

After a long pause she leans into me and says, "You need a new start, Sue, a new adventure. As your friend I'm telling you, you've got to get your life in order. You're angry and it shows. Your energy is terrible. You know how Gordon hates that. Work through this," sipping a glass of Perrier, "I know your career is important to you. Don't let Christopher mess up everything you've worked for. You need to be careful. People are talking."

I'm aware that I've become the office freak, sullen and brooding, growling at designers and nitpicking my team of writers whom Margaret had finally found the money to let me hire. I'm about to turn 40 - with an alarming lack of desk photos of tow-headed kids in snowsuits or adoring husbands beside me on a beach in Hawaii.

My life looks and feels all wrong; my personal failures piling up since the day I'd been widowed at 29.

I still manage my production deadlines flawlessly and crank out satisfying enough issues every month, but inside I feel soulless and hollow.

Months crawl by while I live on empty, taking secret phone calls from Christopher who misses me again and is distraught about what to do about the problem of us.

He flies into town for brief reunions, sweaty and nervous, can't live without you, how can we make this work, tossing and turning at night, calling his children while I shower.

But we know it's unworkable, too many lives at stake, and my anger now seeping out at him, destroying our sweet moments.

And when I drive him to the airport for his final flight home to San Francisco and we pull up to the curb, I get out to hug him but can't let go.

We stand on the sidewalk, both of us suddenly desperate, hanging on to each other, making loud choking sobs that cause passing strangers to look away, until Christopher bends down to get his suitcase and without looking back - walks inside.

It's finally done.

3

FINDING SHAMBHAVA

May 1991: Rollinsville, Colorado

Days go by in a dreamy grief; in the mornings I linger at home staring at the Horse Chestnut tree just outside my bedroom window. I rearrange the room placing my bed so that I can gaze at its enormous century-old branches. Why must I ever get up? Tell me why tree, tell me why. Can't I just live in your arms, roll around inside your hollow spaces, use your branches to ascend high into the sky and live far above this town of too lovely, too happy, too healthy, too perfect and undamaged people?

Such a familiar place this grief is; comforting in its wholeness; nothing to dream of, to get out of bed for; whom was I trying to kid to think that a powerful brilliant man would love me.

My shame runs so deep, deep as a river; I stare into the mirror upon rising and see the unacceptable face, dark heavy eyebrows and French creole nose that never quite fits the smaller bones of the cheeks and chin, the forehead sloping back too quickly, too lower class, not the touch of wealth and grace – just stepped onto a sailboat -regal forehead of my dad's Irish clan; nor the proud wise forehead of my creole female lineage; somehow I came up short of both; the embarrassing child caught in the middle of two opposing gene pools, fulfilling the grandeur of neither; no wonder, no wonder he couldn't love me; falling back into bed crying, will it always be like this? This loneliness and sense of barely, just barely, just barely.

I walk through a town of beauty, athletic stars, trust fund babies; so hard to hide my pain, to not seem vulnerable as I stroll the Boulder Mall crowded with winners and transcendents when I am so clearly a loser; I'm sure that my unworthiness shines through blatantly. What's a person to do when they live in a winning town and suddenly come undone?

So you use your credit card to buy the dresses and jackets to disguise your ugliness, to impress your team of co-workers that you have not actually hit bottom, have not descended completely into hell, are not wounded and incompetent; and to join the health club that helps you pound it all into the floor every night before you go home.

And now your debt is different, not just a debt of worthiness, a debt of soul; so you live anxiously paycheck to paycheck, piling more stress onto the job that you must keep forever now to stall the collectors; and the only ease from grief is when you dress yourself in something that gives you hope again; says maybe someday someone could find you worthy and your life will not be spent in the alone bed, looking up at the wise tree who invites you to climb its lovely arms all the way to the stars, to lose yourself in dreams. And so you do.

You watch *Out of Africa* until you have it memorized; the lovely language of women who try so hard and still lose everything; are handed compasses by unreachable blue eyed men to help them find their way; and yet they're shamed by abandonment simply because they long for love; and still after these losses they dig in, sort coffee beans from dawn till dusk, track expenses late into the night; but in the dark of the night all is burned away, rises up to heaven in billowy coffee scented smoke to reveal that God is coming. Finally. God is coming to deliver us.

And when your once best friend, Monique, the girl you danced in modern dance performances with long ago and who once came to your former house to clean up the bile that had spilled from your dying husband's tubes; the friend who struggled to find love and pay bills just like you did, shows up in your apartment with her perfect new baby and her seamless modern new house on a corner in the suburbs north of here where only happy people live - this house provided by the trust fund husband who adores her - and she doesn't have to work now, never will again, and she looks at you with pity and maybe a little scorn, maybe a little 'see I'm better than you after all' in her tone – telling you that 'in the end we all get exactly what we deserve'; you know now that your only friend will be from this moment on your wounded beloved Margaret who is really the only thing that gets you walking back into that office after all.

And so you rise in the mornings and dress for work in your too costly dresses because you think they hide your pain; help you appear lovely and graceful when certainly you are not. Certainly you are running far below empty and yet without the job there would be no possibility of breath, no connection to this world; and somehow you know that you must stay in this; keep trying until you can't anymore and maybe that day is next week or tomorrow but at least not today. So you get to work just a little late, and your blow-dried hair and heavy eye makeup make it seem that you're still alive.

But the longing simmers just below the pain, blends quietly with the anger and fear as you stroll through the halls pretending to be A-Okay and walk into Allison's office to discuss page layouts.

As you debate the wrap of copy around a photo you suddenly can't take your eyes away from a brochure that's sitting on her desk - even though you should be gazing at the B-Vitamins For Depression article - instead you're staring at the colorful brochure, picking it up, feeling it in your hands, and finally you ask; "What's this?"

"Oh, that's a retreat center just up Boulder canyon," says Allison. "I go there with girlfriends sometimes for the weekend. We do yoga and meditation. You know. Spiritual stuff," smiling at me.

You look through the intriguing brochure. Tight-clad women hold graceful yoga poses on a sunlit wooden deck; tall pine trees blanket a hillside that slopes towards a cozy lake where a canoe rests peacefully on the shore; a large wooden cabin with a pointed blue tin roof dangles rainbow-colored Buddhist prayer flags. You fall in love.

"This is just outside of Boulder?" you ask casually.

"Yeah. Why don't you take the brochure," she offers.

Alone in my office I study the glossy photos,

I'm taken aback by a picture of a large man with kind eyes, a wide generous smile, robed in orange silk, his dark wavy hair pulled sleekly back into a pony tail. He stares directly into the camera.

"Sri Shambhava has nourished the growth of devoted students across the world for over twenty years," reads the brochure. *"His inherent sense of happiness and spiritual understanding...."*

Inherent sense of happiness and spiritual understanding. Those words hold on to me. There's a 3-day meditation retreat this weekend, Memorial Day weekend. And a phone number.

Or I could stay home and hope that Christopher will call.

I pick up the phone on my desk. "I want to register for the weekend meditation retreat," I say to a soft-spoken woman who answers.

"Are you a student of Babaji's? Have you been here before?"

"No. But I *do* know how to meditate."

"I'm sorry. We're full and this is an intensive retreat only for students who've taken classes here before. It's for our advanced students."

"Okay, thank you."

I walk home. Change my clothes to jeans, white t-shirt, running shoes and a fleece jacket; find a map and fill my car with gas.

As the brochure explains, the retreat center is 30 minutes outside of Boulder, in the mountains past Eldora ski resort and down an unmarked mountain trail. I leave home around 4 pm, driving my Honda wagon determinedly up the winding steep

Boulder canyon road, hands tightly gripped around the steering wheel. I will find this place. They will let me in. This will happen.

Driving through the flat lazy sweep of Nederland town, glancing up at the snow crested Indian peaks, then turning uphill again following signs for the ski resort, then passing the resort, more curvy upward roads lined with thick groves of tall pines. There's snow that I can see now between the trees, high altitude cold, turning on my heater.

An hour later, down another unmarked snow crested road that leads nowhere, lost again, sun setting, my head resting on the steering wheel - how bad do you want this Sue?

Hungry, cold and shaky, I turn the car around and try another mysterious turn lined with tall pines crested in snow, opening out into a flat meadow, then a sharp uphill curve and suddenly a silver cattle gate appeared across the road, shimmering slightly in the lingering light.

You are entering Shambhava Mountain Retreat. Please register at the main hall.

I'm a fierce bitch. And I made it.

The sky has darkened into a moonless night and only a small slip of snowy road appears in front of my car as I drive towards the main building where a rustic wooden sign announces: *Registration*

I catch pieces, slivers of people moving like ghosts through the trees, heading towards an elevated cabin, wood smoke curling from its chimney, colored prayer flags flapping cheerily in the high-mountain air.

I park in front of the registration office, and feeling suddenly terrified, walk down the crunchy snow covered path and inside. An attractive man and woman in their 40s with matching steel blue eyes and thick dark hair sit behind a table spread with papers, talking to a woman bundled in a down coat and woolen hat. They whisper and laugh with her like old friends, taking her check and directing her to the meditation cabin.

They turn their gazes towards me and I approach the table more confidently than I feel, "I'm Sue Frederick and I called earlier. I need to be here."

"Hmm, I remember," says the woman looking at her partner who smiles up at me.

His eyes are disturbingly blue as he gazes at me. "Do you meditate?" he asks simply.

"I learned T.M. ten years ago, but I... I need help, I need something more."

Is it my imagination or does he close his eyes and take a deep breath, holding it slightly before exhaling, then opening his eyes again to look at me? "Have you been to our classes before," he asks. "Do you know our teacher?"

"No, but please, I need to be here."

"Okay," with a pause, then warmly, "registration for the weekend is $100. They'll be starting soon in the building next door. You'll stay in the dorm cabin," handing me a map.

I write the check, find a bathroom in the main building - which smells of propane and wood smoke - then head outside to the meditation hall. Thirty or so pairs of shoes, mostly clogs and snow boots, litter the tiny porched entrance to the hall, so I add my running shoes to the pile.

Taking a deep breath, standing just outside the door, I feel like finally, after all of my lost days, my tormented dreams, I'm just now, just this moment, right where I'm supposed to be, finally home, arrived at a place that feels like déjà vu.

Inside dozens of people, wrapped in blankets and shawls, sit on round blue cushions, eyes closed, facing the front of the room. The air is expectant, charged. The pungent scent of sandalwood, myrrh and frankincense mingle with wood smoke from the stove roaring in the back.

I grab a grey woolen blanket and meditation cushion from a stack by the door and find a place in the back. Sitting down I focus on the altar at the front of the room where six-foot-tall golden and bronzed deities stare back at me. They're crowned in white and orange carnations, with too many arms sticking out from their sides, sitting on illuminated lotus blossoms, or there's an enormous elephant trunk where a nose should be. Grey incense smoke rises lazily past their staring faces.

Is the bronzed and bejeweled female statue with four arms looking directly at me? A chill runs down my spine and I close my eyes then slowly open them again.

A large painting hangs on the wall above them; a brown skinned man with short grey hair, clear brown eyes, a slim white goatee and an enormous white cloak wrapping round him and spreading down to the bottom of the painting. He gazes directly at me, his hands protruding out from beneath his cloak, fingers spread apart and shockingly large, disproportionate, the light hitting his fingertips in a way that illuminates them eerily, giving them movement, an inner glow.

Those large illuminated hands spark a memory, something familiar. Have I dreamed about him before?

I hear a rustle at the door and see a woman with long dark and wavy hair leaning down to pick up a cushion then walking slowly to the front of the room where she sits facing us, eyes closed in meditation. She wears a long graceful blue dress with an enormous orange shawl wrapped around her body.

I try to meditate using my T.M. mantra: Shhremmm, a long hushed sounding word that I'd repeated everyday since I'd turned 30 and been initiated.

Eventually she speaks to the group, "Thank you for coming everyone," she's sweet and pretty, not what I expected, soft and sensual, unflinchingly lovely.

"This will be an auspicious weekend," she says glancing across the room at our faces. "We'll peel away old layers that we no longer need using breath and mantra to experience what lies beyond the mind, opening up to the powerful cleansing energy of Nityananda, our guru. Our teacher, Babaji, will be here soon to guide us. He's excited about a new meditation technique that he's eager to share with you. In the meantime, let's begin chanting to clear the energy in the room and help you remove whatever holds you back."

Someone behind me begins playing a few bars on an organ-sounding keyboard and slowly the entire room begins singing in unison *Om Namah Shivaya*. The singing rises and falls around me mournfully then longingly, stirring up a deep grief, not for what I'd lost, but for who I have become.

After 30 minutes or so, the door opens and Babaji enters, a bustle of orange silk robes sashaying, weaving through the rows of chanters, reaching down to tap someone sharply on their head as he passes, that person falling over into a spasm.

I feel the energy in the room sharpen, the chanting grows louder, people around me inhale deeply, some moan and a few seem to pass out, falling over backwards from their cushions. Babaji stops beside the lovely woman who'd been speaking to us from the front of the room; his hand presses hard into the top of her head while she leans back, inhaling sharply, gazing up at him, then exhaling and crumbling backwards to the floor.

Babaji arranges his large generous body cloaked in orange silk to sit facing us from an ornate couch, velvet cushioned and curvy, his legs tucked beneath him on the cushions. I can't take my eyes away.

As the organ draws to a slow finish and the room quiets, I'm looking into the eyes of a man who seems familiar. I'd seen his face in the brochure, but, this man, laughing merrily, looking around the room at us, waving and smiling broadly, focusing on me for a brief instant, isn't he an old boyfriend from the 70s? Isn't this Jerry from my days in the commune?

Look again. No, that isn't Jerry, but someone so familiar, and now he's speaking in a deep voice, rich, powerful and melodious, a rock star or an actor. No, that isn't it. And for a brief second he seems to look like Christopher, soft, round and sweetly sensual, telling me he loves me.

My mind is scrambled, confused. I feel dizzy but alive, awake, thrilled and terrified.

For a moment, he focuses his gaze above our heads to the wall behind us, as if conversing silently with someone hovering in the air above us. Then he shuts his eyes and the room falls back into silent meditation.

Babaji's deep voice eventually breaks the silence: "Bring your breath deep within, hold it, then circulate it through your chakras, feel it loosening up the blocks inside of you, releasing your Kundalini, uncoiling it up your spine, then out the top of your head."

Beside me, people inhale and exhale loudly, circulating their breath, I guess. So I try it, inhaling deeply through my nose, moving the air down inside, past my throat, through my stomach, around and through my sex organs, then up through my spine, exhaling, imagining breath moving out through the top of my head. I feel a sudden and fierce rush of energy, a tingle, almost sexual in nature, startling and awakening.

We practice this silently for almost an hour. I return to my T.M. mantra whenever it feels like too much, too strange. People in the room continue to gasp and topple over around me. I try to ignore them.

Babaji stands up again, walking slowly amidst the students, touching their heads, patting some sharply, others tenderly, looking up at something above us, inhaling deeply, then brushing his hand from the top of one student's head down the front of her body, an unzipping motion. She moans, gasps and falls over backwards.

Babaji approaches me. I can't stop looking at him. He puts his hand gently, briefly on my head, our eyes lock, then he turns and walks out the door. The woman in the front of the room leads us through another round of chanting while tears stream down my cheeks, I sniffle, then sob, feeling like a fool, unable to stop crying.

When the chanting ends, she tells us to soak up the sweetness, the nectar of our Guru Nityananda, motioning towards the painting above her head of the man with illuminated hands. "Let the work we've done today continue to open our hearts. Namaste," and she's gone. People get up slowly, shuffling out the door to find their shoes and trudge quietly back to their cabins. It's a silent retreat, I'd learned, no talking allowed.

That night I dream of my departed husband Paul, pale and thin in my arms, then Christopher's soft lips kissing me, then later, Babaji walking slowly down a staircase to a room where I await, arms wide open.

I wake in the dark, running for the door, longing for my apartment and begging Christopher to come back to me.

4

ARE THERE ANY QUESTIONS?

May 1991: Rollinsville, Colorado

The morning bell rings. No sunlight outside. Someone turns on the ceiling light. My dorm mates pad silently to the bathroom.

Shaking away my dreams of elephant heads and a towering man with huge hands hitting me on the head, I sit on my bunk.

I need coffee. Will they have coffee? Some one in the bunk beside mine smiles and hugs me while we wait our turn for a shower.

In the dining hall, I eat hot rice cereal and drink black tea. My stomach feels queasy, so I find the bathroom that smells of propane and wood smoke and gulp a few Ginger capsules. Staring into the dim mirror I say, "You can do this. You need this."

"How did you sleep?" asks the lovely dark-haired woman from yesterday's class who's standing outside the bathroom when I emerge. Was she waiting for me? She smiles warmly, her eyes are blue of course; blue indigo pools that I try not to fall into as she continues, "If you're doing this work correctly, your ego will rally with all sorts of reasons you shouldn't do it, telling you to run, that things are fine just as they are."

She has me cornered against the bathroom door. "Hi my name is Faith, and I'm Babaji's wife. He wants me to tell you that he's glad you're here. He likes your energy. Says you're a good meditator."

She laughs and hugs me, her luxurious thick wavy hair pressing against my face smelling of rose oil and sandalwood, pushing her generous chest into mine to hold it there while she takes a deep breath. Then pulling away and looking into my eyes with something that feels genuine; concern or maybe just curiosity.

"Well, I ran out of the cabin last night in a panic attack and spent awhile sitting on the porch outside, freezing my butt off. I guess my ego was rallying to battle."

We both laugh. I smile and extend my hand, "Hi, I'm Sue. I'm amazed and overwhelmed by what I experienced yesterday. It feels kinda wonderful and kinda terrifying. I'm glad I came."

"This is your first time to Shambhava, right? It's a lot to take in."

"I'll say."

"You'll find that your dreams are quite intense up here because of the energy from our gurus, our lineage. It's purifying you. Can even make you feel a little sick."

"Well then I'm right on schedule," I smile showing her my bottle of Ginger capsules, making her laugh again.

"Christopher and Elizabeth say they let you in last night because of your determination. And your energy. They'd already turned you down on the phone, right?" She giggles. "And you came all the way up here anyway? That's something. Babaji likes students who are hungry for the work."

"I'm hungry indeed," I say, giggling with her. She's intoxicating, warm and insistently lovely. She looks to be around my age. I want to know her, hear her story, find out how she ended up here living this life. And is it a coincidence or a sign that the blue-eyed man who'd let me in last night was named Christopher?

The gong rings outside, calling us to the meditation cabin. "I'm here if you want to talk. And don't be afraid to ask questions today during class. I'm glad you've come," she says turning to go.

Back in the meditation cabin, another round of chanting, Faith leading us through more meditation, circling breath through our chakras, and finally the bustling of orange robes and Babaji's bright entrance like a flame, igniting the room.

Sitting in the front of the room facing us, Babaji stares at the air above our heads again having his moment with the unseen deity, then asks: "Are there any questions?"

A woman beside me says, "Babaji, when I circulate the breath around and through my chakras it always gets stuck in my solar plexus and I feel like I've hit a wall. I can't move the energy past there."

Babaji looks off into the distance again. After awhile he says, "You've spent your life hiding from your true self. It's so powerful that you're afraid of it. If you faced it, owned it, you would have to change your life and change all of your relationships. That's the fear you're hitting against when you meditate. Your solar plexus is blocked from fear of being powerful."

They exchange comments back and forth for awhile, but I'm not listening. Babaji had spoken to me, only me, when he answered that student's question.

I'd spent my life hiding from my true self. Choosing instead to be the perfectly stifled, obedient Catholic child, then the angry rebellious hippie daughter, the fierce wife of a dying man, the journalist who chose her career mainly from a sense of failure to become a true writer, and finally the sad woman who gave her soul away to a married man.

None of that was me. The essence of me. And I understood that. But I didn't know how to find the essence of me.

"You. In the white shirt. "

Babaji is looking directly at me.

"Me?" I ask timidly, my voice suddenly weak and unsure, clearing my throat, "My name is Sue."

"Welcome to our Sangha. You're new and you're a good meditator. You've found your seat. You must have meditated before. Your energy is good." He smiles his glorious blazing smile, shimmering in my eyes like burnt sienna, confusing me, don't I know him from somewhere?

Finding my voice, "Yes Babaji. I've done T.M. meditation before. But this is all new to me."

"Maybe it's new to you in this lifetime. But not new to YOU. You've done this work before. Do you have any questions?"

"I have so much sadness coming up. What do I do with it? Where does it come from? And what happened to me yesterday when you tapped my head?"

I watch him circulate his breath through his chakras, looking up again into the space above us then saying: "Let the sadness come up and release it with your breath. You've had a lot of loss. It doesn't matter why it's there or where it came from. Mantra and breath will move it out of you."

I feel tears rolling down my cheeks. "I gave you Shaktipat yesterday," he adds softly. "It's a spiritual energy cleanser. Kundalini energy. It's cleaning you out."

"Oh. Wow. Thank you! I needed that. Spiritual Draino. Thank you Babaji. It's working," I say laughing and sniffling. "What else should I do to help the process?"

"Just meditate. And love Nityananda." He points to the photo on the wall above his head, to the tall guy who'd hit me on the head with his enormous hands in my dreams.

And so my relationship with my teacher begins.

I become a weekend yogi, trudging through my workweek at New Times with a more loving demeanor and counting the hours until my Friday evening escape to Shambhava Mountain Retreat. But my heart still longs for a man.

So it's no surprise to me months later when Babaji calls me in to the Ashram sunroom one Saturday morning to talk about a grey cloud of grief he sees hovering around me. I sit on a meditation cushion at his feet, looking up him, trying not to cry.

"It's lighter than when you first arrived, it's breaking up now from your Kundalini work. I can use Shaktipat to push it away, but if you don't change your inner self, it comes back," he says kindly, his fingers moving deftly across the beads of his coral mala, his presence large and luminous and unsettlingly beautiful to me.

Of course I'm in love with him. It's part recognition of him as my teacher. Something I'd read about in spiritual books, the way you fall in love with your teacher so that you'll be open to the lessons.

And it's the way he morphs from Christopher to Paul to my father whenever he looks at me, becoming all the men who have ever loved me, but now glorious and evolved, compassionate and forgiving. And not mine.

I take a deep breath, circulating it to the base of my spine and through my chakras the way I'd learned in class. "I'm meditating everyday Babaji. And I do the breath circulations, the Kundalini work. What else should I do?"

"Life ain't easy for a girl named Sue," he laughs, twisting the lines from an old Johnny Cash song of the 60s, his voice kind and playful, his smile luminous. "You're still holding on to Christopher - to people and illusions you need to surrender."

This was true. I still dreamed of Christopher, heard his name mentioned too often in industry meetings. I knew it was a matter of time before I ran into him at one of our expos.

"I want a family, children, the white picket fence, a porch with wicker furniture. This longing makes me unhappy."

"You must surrender all of that. It's fleeting," he says waving his hand. "What endures is your inner self, your true nature, that's all you have and you carry it with you wherever you go," laughing then his face softening as he leans towards me. "Just keep meditating, honey. You'll be fine. Stay away from Christopher. And love Nityananda. The grief, the grey cloud, will dissipate."

"And forget about the white picket fence dream?"

"Don't focus on that. Focus within, on your breath, on your mantra. If those other things are meant to be, they will. But not by you pursuing them or focusing on them. Discipline of the mind, of the inner self, is essential," his large hands waving towards to photo of Nityananda above him. "Focus on Nityananda whenever you find yourself longing for the white picket fence. And forget your past. Release it with each breath."

He leans forward to hug me briefly and waves me off.

His energy makes me feel dizzy, light-headed, cleaned out just from sitting near him or from the sound of his deep rich voice; I'm entranced.

I bow to the ground in front of him and walk outside to do my weekend Seva, selfless work. This time I'm assigned to build trails with other weekend volunteers from Boulder, Denver and elsewhere – all of us escaping lives that seem not enough, looking for a richness that we find here in this community, doing spiritual practice and hauling rocks to forget.

How strangely beautiful I feel in these smudged and stained mirrors, in the dimly lit rooms with soft light falling in through the windows, my face looks tender, gentle when I see it in a reflection; hair dirty and simple; eyeliner smeared and disappearing; I feel lovely as we walk the rugged land; none of us pretending to be perfect or even better than; all of us meeting on some kind of common ground; maybe a different dimension, or maybe we're all "caught-betweens" - caught between two genetic lines of perfection and we fall somewhere in the middle with gifts that are strange and not valued in a linear world, yet here we lift rocks and cry and tell stories we would never tell in the city or on the lovely mall of Boulder; and with our stories we wash each other's feet and humble ourselves to the great big open-hearted man we call Babaji.

Yet when I drive home, down the twisting canyon road and enter my apartment she's still there – the flawed girl; but maybe she only lives on the outside now, in my reflection, and maybe someone better is being birthed inside; and someday she will shine through, break through the cracks in the mirror and emerge; and I will find myself beautiful inside and out. Just maybe.

5

Old Trouble in New Times

Summer 1991: Boulder Colorado

Gordon is mostly gone from the office now, traveling the world with his new young girlfriend. New Times' pockets have grown rich and spilling over; our three different magazines (New Times also published a trade journal for the natural foods industry and a trade journal for the relocation industry) are flourishing and our fabulously attended Expos have tripled in size.

Margaret has been promoted to President of the entire corporation and handed the daily running of the company. Yet her relationship with Gordon suffers from the day she takes the reins. She steps eagerly into her new role, holding productive meetings with each department, hiring much-needed staff, and taking control of things she's long wanted to change. But Gordon questions her decisions - especially around budgetary matters, holding long conference calls with Margaret and Cinda the CFO - from his faraway travels in Africa, New Zealand, Amsterdam.

New Times feels more solid to most of its employees who fear the wrath of Gordon. But to me, it has become tricky. My visits with Gordon are few and far between. I miss him and our wild conversations. And my friendship with Margaret has shifted. She's struggling to find her voice as the president of a million-dollar company with now more than 100 employees - 30% of them men. She's come on strong from the beginning of her new role, wanting to establish her authority over the many factions of a dysfunctional company.

But there are grumblings, angry discontent men questioning if she's up for the task. No one doubts her brilliance. But some of the men doubt her experience in the natural foods world and many question her authority.

"Sam challenges me in every meeting. He questions all of my decisions," she complains over coffee at our favorite café. Sam is editor of the trade journal for the natural foods industry and has been with the company longer than Margaret, clearly hoping for a big promotion. When Margaret got the job, Sam's disappointment took the form of sabotaging comments behind her back and argumentative confrontations during meetings.

"You're handling it just right, Margaret. You're not pushing too hard yet you come across as strong and confident," I say leaning across the table. "I'm in awe of how you handle yourself. You're doing great."

"Oh honey, I don't know," she has tears in her eyes.

She tells me she's lonely and unsure about her new role. Her new responsibilities mean that she and I seldom travel together and she spends her time nurturing a new sales team of mostly men – pushing them to meet lofty sales goals and keep the magazines on track. She has to oversee company budgets and Expo planning and her personal life is in shambles, with another fleeting and painful relationship coming to an end.

When I tell her briefly about my time at the Ashram she isn't enthusiastic about it. "Well, if it makes you feel better that's great. Are you sure it isn't a cult?"

We are slowly, silently growing apart; I spend my extra time and every weekend at the Ashram and she spends hers alone or on dates that leave her feeling empty. She feels that I've pushed her out of my life when I began my work at Shambhava, and this hurts her deeply. And I feel judged by her whenever I share my latest conversation with Babaji.

And I have, without realizing it, become more powerful. In meetings, I speak my truth without backing down when others disagree. Yet I'm not angry like before, someone to pity, instead I'm becoming something new, something I don't quite recognize; confident and fearless, unconcerned with the opinions of others, no longer desperate for love.

This is dangerous behavior at New Times. I can see it makes everyone uncomfortable, even Margaret. Gordon believes that our magazines should be run by consensus, forcing us to rule by committee. We're told to include opinions from all departments when planning our annual editorial calendars. The opinions of Andrew from shipping or Dara from Human Resources are taken as seriously as the insights from my own team of writers who devote 24/7 to the magazine.

This is disheartening to me and to my team, so I decide, after a few months of working with Babaji, that I won't do editorial meetings that way anymore. I make a decision to have the next one at Shambhava Mountain Retreat and anyone who doesn't want to come doesn't have to.

"Sue, you can't do that. It's a long drive and half the people can't even make it," says Margaret.

"That's perfect."

"Sue, you just can't do things this way."

"Why not? We'll have a very productive meeting up there, like a retreat, and everyone does not need to attend."

"Babaji, I'm sort of stirring up trouble at my job," I say one night at Satsang, all of us gathered around on meditation cushions as he takes our questions.

He smiles and laughs, "Of course, of course. It's the Shaktipat opening you up. Sometimes trouble is a good thing," a long pause while he communes with Nityananda.

"Yes the energy brings everything to the surface to be looked at. You're being asked to step into your power in ways you haven't before. But be careful. It's a tricky situation there. Be sure you know what you want."

What do I want? That isn't clear to me. But I feel like my old skin is shedding and my new true self is emerging raw, tender and fierce. I'm becoming someone I barely recognize.

On the day I'm called into a meeting in the art director's office I sense what's coming. As the company's Art Director, Jane answers to Margaret and not to me. Whenever I reject Jane's design ideas for the magazine page layouts (which I do frequently now) or don't like a cover mock-up, she tells me I'm difficult and overstepping my role as Editor.

Sitting down at the conference table, it's quickly clear that this meeting is about me. My solar plexus, what Babaji calls my power center, is doing cartwheels and my heart rate doubles the instant I enter the room. After I sit down and Margaret makes nervous small talk without meeting my eyes, she launches into the purpose of the meeting.

"Sue, Jane and several designers and some of your editorial team, and Sam and his team from Natural Products Merchandiser think you're being too difficult lately," Margaret's movements are exaggerated, hand brushing the hair back too many times, clearing her throat, never quite able to meet my eyes.

"Yes Sue," says Jane, smiling broadly, crossing her hands on the table, diamond wedding band glimmering in the fluorescent lights. "I have 20 years experience as a designer and I don't feel like you let me implement my vision," arching her eyebrows in sympathy, "I know you've been through so much Sue," voice sweet as sugar, "but you have very strong opinions and you're difficult to work with."

Other people in the room nod in agreement and slowly they go around the table outlining how I've made decisions without them, or made demands on them that seem unreasonable.

I fight back tears and focus on the inner vision of Nityananda as Babaji had taught me to do. I quietly move my breath through my chakras before speaking. I realize that Babaji has warned me about this happening. He's often said that when serious students begin doing true spiritual work that it brings up all of their unresolved karma to be dealt with. In other words, the shit hits the fan. This is my shit hitting the fan.

"Well, it all comes down to who is really in charge of the magazine, doesn't it?" I ask, keeping my voice flat. "Am I the editor or not? Do I get fired if the magazine fails or does Jane, the art director? I believe the editor is the one in charge and the one who gets fired if it fails. This magazine can't be run by committee. That's not how it's done."

"Two of your writers say you're too demanding, Sue," fires back Margaret.

"I bet they do," I smile at her. "I now demand they show up, do their work and meet their deadlines, something they aren't used to here."

After an hour of confrontive discussion back and forth, it's over. I feel betrayed by Margaret and diminished by Jane. Margaret has sided with the others in the meeting when it was her place to side with the editor, as I see it, the one in charge of the magazine's ultimate success or failure. They've intimidated me, using their awareness of my weak spots to hurt me.

My staff and I have known for awhile that the hierarchy Gordon implemented long ago was dysfunctional. Each magazine needs its own art director who answers only to that publication's editor. Instead, Jane oversees all publications and answers only to Gordon - and now Margaret.

Jane and I have gone head to head many times and this meeting is no exception. "Jane most of your design experience is with packaging and marketing materials," I say trying to keep my voice low and calm. "That's very different from art directing a consumer magazine that needs to be readable and compelling. I get feedback from our readers everyday about how people like or don't like our covers. And they mostly don't like them."

"Sue, you've never been editor of a magazine before, have you?" asks Jane, smiling graciously. "Maybe you should listen to us more. Quit being so defensive. We just want to help you," eyebrows raised in sympathy, head tilted.

I feel deeply hurt, yet a calmer part of me feels unshaken, alive, observing the attack from a detached and almost amused viewpoint. If this is the result of becoming more powerful in my workplace, then it's a moment to step into the next level of my inner work and not crumble – as I always have before.

I return to my office and sit behind my desk trying not to cry, feeling bruised and like the breath has been knocked out of me. I stare at the small photo of Nityananda on my desk, carefully circulating the breath through my chakras, calming myself down ever so slowly. Asking Nityananda to fill me with something, wisdom and courage maybe.

There's a knock on my door and one of my editorial staff members enters. She wasn't at the meeting but has already heard the gossip in the halls. As a fellow meditator and student of Guru Mai (who came from the same lineage as my Babaji) we've bonded in recent weeks; sharing our experiences, our wonder at the work we're doing.

"Do you think you'll get fired?" she whispers.

"I think I need to be kinder and gentler."

She laughs out loud. "Sure you do, Sue. But do you think a man would say that if he'd just come out of a meeting like that? Hell no!" she breaks down in giggles, wrapping her arms around me. Soon we're laughing out loud, doubled over in hysteria at the absurdity of the job, the company, this world; hanging on to each other, tears streaming down our faces. "You need to sneak out of here right now and go commune with Nityananda," she says handing me my purse. "I'll cover you," she opens my office door to peak down the hall. "All clear."

By the time I walk home to my apartment the world has rearranged itself into a blur of wavy flickering orange and yellow lightning bolts; a migraine. I call my acupuncturist. He agrees to see me.

"So they're going after you now because you're powerful," he says as he places needles in my temples, wrists and ankles. Of course, of course, his eyes are stupid blue, wonderful blue, and he is gifted, brilliant, magnificent and perfectly married.

"Or because I'm terrible," I say.

He sits on a chair in the corner of the room while I lay still on the table; eyes closed, observing the flashing bolts of light shimmer and quiver behind my eyelids. A Zen fountain gurgles from the hallway; he's thoughtful and quiet, then asks:

"Why do you get migraines?"

"Because I'm disgusted with the world and don't want to see it anymore."

"Or because you need to change the way you look at things; change your point of view."

"Right. Bingo. Workin' on that."

"You know Sue, those places, especially New Times, they're all one big power game; it doesn't matter what good things the company does for the world; what goes on inside is always the same; people stepping over each other to climb to the top. You just have to know what you want."

"Same thing Babaji says."

"Maybe you should listen to us."

"David, are you kidding me; I listen to every word you say; it's why I'm here right now on your table letting you torture me."

He laughs. "Well do you know what you want?"

"Yes; do we always get what we want David?"

"Quit giving away your energy, your chi. Just focus on centering and grounding," he says leaning over me to remove the needles; the flashing lines of color already fading, muscles in my neck releasing.

"You know all of this already, Sue. Quit being such a baby." He smiles and leaves the room.

Later that night, meditating alone in my apartment, I'm aware of feeling powerful, not vulnerable – my usual reaction to confrontation. This is new for me, not something I've ever felt as far back as I can remember.

This time I see the truth of the moment; feel Nityananda's wisdom filling me up, spreading out into the empty corners, the dark spaces of self-doubt. This is the price of speaking my truth – not everyone will like it. I need to take Gordon's management approach – fire the magazine's staff members who don't like the new me - and hire ones that do.

That thought makes me laugh out loud – such a controversial move to make in a company dominated by women who care passionately about pleasing each other. It could cause all the cards of my career to come tumbling down. But I know I've found my core strength – the fruits of my spiritual practice blossoming.

Finally I'm becoming more in alignment with my powerful wise soul than my wounded ego. To do my job and create a great magazine I can't give a shit what anyone at New Times thinks of me. And I can't give a shit if I ever see Christopher or fall in love again. It's done. All of it finished. The old me, my pitiful self, peeling away.

It's a sleepless night and I spend most of it gazing at my Horse Chestnut Tree; at one point I'm lifted into the branches and have the hospital dream; the one where I'm running through the hallways trying to escape and every door leads into another room of suffering people; and when I stop to help someone he crumbles in my arms and his suffering gets worse and I run until I'm lost in a hallway of surgeries; bodies cut open, blood and bile everywhere; and I can't find my way out; can never find the exit door and finally wake up panting, sweating, my God why, why this dream again when I think I'm finally good, Teflon-coated, healed, strong enough, good enough; why I ask Nityananda, why this dream? And when my eyes close again and I lift into one final sleep before the alarm, I'm in Long Beach on the front porch beside my father who looks very content as we watch summer squalls moving across the choppy water.

To prepare for our first editorial calendar meeting at Shambhava Mountain retreat, Faith and I stay up late in the dining hall the night before. "I'll lead them through a heart opening meditation to begin the morning," she whispers, sipping hot and milky chai tea, the cloves permeating the air around us, making notes on her yellow pad. "What time do they arrive?"

"At 10 am if they don't get lost."

"They won't. I'll ask Nityananda to get them here on time," she laughs softly, her face stretching into a brilliant smile, closing her eyes briefly to circulate her breath. "After meditation, we'll serve a light breakfast, something corporate but nice, like quiche and coffee?" she looks up me. I nod.

"Don't be nervous. The energy here will clean out the negativity," she whispers, putting her warm hand on top of mine. "We'll dose the food with extra love."

The next day, standing in front of a huge white board that Brian, one of the meditation teachers, sets up in the dining hall, I study the enormous group, every department of New Times represented, the air charged with sweetness, sparked from the moment they arrived and Faith began the meditation.

Closing my eyes for a second, inhaling, communing with Nityananda, then ringing the gong to begin the meeting, I feel alive, on purpose, excited to share our editorial ideas for the coming year, our content already clarified through weeks of hard work with my staff. The group is mostly quiet, listening, nodding; offering small suggestions here and there. Jane isn't at the meeting. Margaret nods approval at all of my ideas.

We make lightning progress through the usually tedious agenda, with Faith stepping in to quietly serve snacks and Chai tea, the room thick with the scent of cinnamon and cloves. She turns to smile at me, her energy lighting up the hall, before slipping back into the kitchen.

The long day shifts something for me at New Times, deep inside. I'm clearly different now at work, gracefully firing and hiring staff, surrounding myself with brilliant funny women who work harder than I ever ask them to.

Saturday morning 8 AM. My hiking boots are on. I'm in town for the weekend because the magazine is on deadline and there are page proofs to finalize. My Saturdays in Boulder always start with this hike up Sanitas Ridge.

Today Margaret plans to join me. I see her as I round the corner from Mapleton to the trailhead of Sanitas. She's parking her car and I wait.

"Hi darlin," she says, all smiles and hugs, her day pack dangling from her hand, bending down to adjust the laces on her hiking boots, then straightening to pull her hair into a short ponytail. "I've got so much to tell you!" laughing and giggling, breathless as Marilyn Monroe; the Margaret I love.

The hike is steep and rocky. I'm winded in the beginning as we round the sandstone walls where climbers, hands painted with white chalk, balance on rock nubbins high above us. Years ago I was one of those rock dancers, dressed in snug sticky shoes, running my fingers lovingly over carabiners and wired stopper cams; craving the feel of the cold rock against my skin much like I now crave the feel of my rosewood mala beads.

We continue past them, the trail smelling of sulphur and granite dust, crushed yarrow and Artemisia. We hike silently side by side. Years of hiking this trail together we take it on like an Everest summit. No resting except for water breaks. The sun bears down on us as the trail rounds the corner and swings to the east of the ridge. We know where we're going. The sound of our heavy breathing is the only sound we make. One foot in front of the other no matter how steep it gets.

Other hikers move aside to let us pass, guzzling from their water bottles, enjoying the Boulder skyline; its downward slope pushing away from these hills, spilling far into the flatlands of eastern Colorado and beyond.

In 20 minutes we've gained 1,000 feet of altitude and we're still climbing strong. I love her intensity. We are uncannily matched for hiking; Margaret with her rounded curves, her voluptuousness; me with my straight arrow lines and tightly wound muscles. We look crazy different. But our determination is perfectly in sync. We never invite friends to hike with us; it's too tedious.

After 30 minutes of straight up silent hiking, we round the ridge to see a glimpse of our secret basin nestled high near the peak of the ridge, facing west into the wide-open vista of the

Rocky Mountains; a startling view of Long's Peak reaching sharply into distant clouds, white snow icing its jagged summit.

We slip behind the pine trees and between the large boulders and sink happily into our private basin of sandstone formed by thousands of years of snow, ice and water -holding us sacred and warm, facing the afternoon sun. We share chocolate, nuts and water.

"You go first," I say.

"Oh Sue, it's kinda wild. And wonderful. I've been going to these parties, it's hard to explain," she sighs, still breathless from the hike, pausing, perhaps deciding how much to share; taking a moment to suck more water from her bottle.

She turns to face me, "There's this group. They have a teacher. They have all-night parties on Friday nights at someone's house. It's very exclusive and I got invited. At first I didn't know what to make of it. We dance all night, with everyone. And then we all sleep with different partners; everyone has sex!" she laughs out loud and leans her head back on the rock, eyes closed, giggling.

"I know it sounds insane, but it's kinda wonderful," she whispers, looking off into the distant sky, billowy clouds hovering above the summit of distant peaks, far from where we sit warm and toasty in the sun. "In the mornings we eat breakfast with our teacher," she continues. "We talk about love, attachment, connection. I'm learning about jealousy and fearless love, about personal power. Oh it's all so good Sue," she looks over at me, taking my hand. "There's just too much to explain."

"I'm listening. Tell me more," I plead, "This is good, really good."

She laughs, looks at me and nods. We both sit quietly, munching on roasted almonds, silent for awhile. I'm picturing Margaret in this group; watch her dancing wildly, losing her self-consciousness, picking a partner for the night without doubting herself; without feeling left out, unwanted or uninteresting; the way her powerful family made her feel growing up – the child who wasn't creative like the older siblings, like the father who was a tycoon of the advertising industry in the 60s – the genius who sucked the air from a room with his large presence, his cruel and funny brilliance, his violent alcoholic rages.

"Wow," I whisper. "This is great for you. I see it. I understand it."

She sits up, away from the warm rock, looks directly at me, "It's so good Sue. So terribly weird and unconventional, but so good for me. I feel good about myself. And powerful with men. Instead of, you know, the way I've been."

"I know. I understand." As we talk more about it, I hear the details of the networking in the group, the sleeping arrangements, how their teacher picks partners for them, how they eat a strict diet of unprocessed foods and only eat meals at certain times, how they're required to run at least three miles together everyday but it becomes six and then ten and now she's doing maybe 13 a day.

"Oh my God Margaret I love this. We're both having such powerful experiences in very different ways - but they're still the same," I take her hand. "I know," she says, dark eyes glistening. "I knew you'd understand."

We sit quietly snacking on chocolate, drinking water. I think about my weekends at the ashram doing intense inner work, long meditations, hard physical labor, thoughtful conversations with my teacher; getting up before sunrise each morning, cold and sleepy to join the early morning hour-long Guru Gita chanting meditation. I see Margaret at her wild parties, discussing love and jealousy in the mornings with her teacher. It's all the same lesson, perfectly designed for our very different lives.

"What we're learning is the same," laughs Margaret. "How cool is that?"

I agree. When the talk turns to New Times she tells me that she's changing the management structure and that Jane will no longer be involved in my magazine's art direction. I'll appoint a new art director from the pool of designers that Jane once managed. That new person, the new art director, will answer directly to me.

The painful, bullying meeting from months ago is never mentioned; our friendship having come to its own alignment, quietly and gracefully.

We talk until the sun slips into the western horizon, painting the rocks orange; the air chills quickly, western winds sweeping in from distant peaks, pushing our warmth away, far down the rocky slopes towards Kansas.

6

LIFTING THE VEIL

July 1980 – Ten years earlier in Boulder Colorado

It's 2am. No sleep. Wrapped in a sheet upstairs on the floor on my camping mat, knowing something but not wanting to know it, how Paul's eyes were distant, the conversations vague, his thin arms too painful to look at, his soul already traveling.

I'd just hired a nurse to come from midnight until 4 am. That was all I could afford but I thought four hours of sleep might help. Might. Not sure.

The nurse was calling me now from downstairs, from Paul's bed, our bed, now a hospital bed in our living room, which had become a hospital room, decorated with clear bags of IV fluid stacked neatly against the bright yellow bags of Paul's new liquid diet called TPN that I insert through a tube in his chest everyday.

Our bookshelves, that once housed Hemingway and climbing magazines, are stacked with piles of unopened syringes, plastic tubing and bottles of morphine. The endless drone of an NG tube sucking bile from Paul's stomach into a canister floods my ears as I pause in the doorway; rumpled and tired, hesitating, still wearing yesterday's stained tank top and gym shorts. Paul looks up at me, eyes still vivid blue through the morphine. He smiles and lifts a hand to motion me beside him.

"He's throwing up blood and I can't stop it," says the night nurse. "Think you should call your hospice nurse Gwen." She looks flustered, scared.

Paul holds my hand, reaches his other arm around my shoulder, pulls my head gently into his chest, strokes my hair, "Call Gwen," he whispers calmly.

She comes right over, takes pulses and measurements, talks to Paul. She dials 911 and an ambulance arrives in the middle of the night, sirens blaring, waking the neighbors. I pile into the back with Paul and the medic. Paul lifts his hand to wave at his shiny red motorcycle in the parking lot. "Bye motorcycle," he whispers. My stomach churns as we pull away.

At the hospital, Gwen tells me to stay in the ER waiting room. But I never do that. I always stand beside Paul, explaining meds, diagnoses, previous procedures. But not tonight. I can barely stand up.

Slumping into a chair in the waiting room, I dream of a green summer field and a golden light, then Paul beside me wearing his favorite mountaineering jacket, a coiled climbing rope in his hands; he cheers, pumps his arms up and down, points to something in the distance, a snow-capped summit, we're standing on it side-by-side, his hand is warm in mine, puffy grey clouds rising suddenly between us. "Wake up, Sue, wake up," Gwen's voice drags me back in, startles me awake; I jolt upright in the chair. "We have to go upstairs," she whispers, pulling me along behind her.

We drift through hallways, my soul barely with me, my body hardly solid; more liquid than flesh. I'm not having this moment, never wanted this ending. It's not what we fought for. This is all a lie and I don't accept it. I feel nauseous.

In the room Paul is awake. "They stopped the bleeding," says Gwen, adjusting his I.V. Paul pulls me down on the bed beside him, wraps his arms around me, says he left his body in the ER. "Painful procedure," he whispers. "Glad you weren't there to see it. I looked down and saw my body on the table. Felt okay to leave. But I came back for you." He looks at me and says softly, "It's time now Sue."

He wraps his legs around mine. We kiss and cuddle. He tells me I'm gifted. Magical. We touch everywhere that can be caressed without pain. "You'll be fine Sue," he whispers, "Don't waste your life grieving for me. Get married and have babies." His finger points at me, emphasizing a future without him, clear ocean eyes. His gaze already heaven bound.

Hours drag by with too many conversations between Gwen and me, between Gwen and the doctors. "This isn't how he wanted to die," I plead. "He wants the IVs disconnected. Let me take him home."

People appear in the room from nowhere, holding Paul's hand, taking me to the cafeteria where the smell of food rises up inside, a tidal wave of nausea. Friends sit along his bed, line the walls of our room. His mother suddenly arrives from Oklahoma; Paul cries when he sees her standing at the bed holding flowers and orange balloons; cheerful as ever, tidying up the room; she hugs me over and over, sits on his bedside holding a bible; they share whispered conversations and more tears.

Somewhere in the brightness of late afternoon, IVs disconnected finally, he slips slowly into the rhythmic breathing of a deep coma; the sound of his struggled breath fills the room, sends me running to dry heave in a trashcan.

Time collapses, falls in on itself, I feel the same moment repeating endlessly; people seem to come and go from the room, transparent as ghosts, talking too loudly, adjusting things, asking questions about fluids, morphine, taking notes. None of it seems to apply to me. I let it all drift away, my breath rising up and falling down in the same rhythm as Paul's.

Night sneaks in through the window, darkening the room, our faces glow strangely from the fluorescent bed lamp; his mother takes my hand to pray. Later I get up from the bed to stretch, realize I'm dizzy and sick, slide down the wall to sit on the floor; her prayers a low hum in the background, his breathing unchanged; a mourning dove calls from a tree as I fall asleep beside the bed.

How did I get to this moment of losing everything? Did I know he would die when we met under a streetlamp after a day of rock climbing? I did not recognize it, even though the evening light created a halo around his head as he took my hand. I thought he was my savior; he seemed so strong, full of life. Long's Peak was his playground.

I fell into him, he into me. We merged; it was effortless, too much so; perhaps I should have known there were no happy endings, really. But I didn't truly know that, didn't understand how things are.

A few stomach pains led to a world of doctors and hospitals; pulled us away from mountains, remote cabins and climbing friends. We were pretty and strong, people were jealous, and then we were sad and sick, emaciated, and people looked away, had better things to do; went climbing while we sat in heavily air conditioned hospital rooms learning new words like ileostomy, Cisplatinum, adhesions. We were determined, would win this one, overcome the odds; we tried Laetrile, Vitamin C, enzymes, had major surgeries, got chemo, puked in pots, got rebirthed, saw medicine men in South Dakota, changed our diets completely; our stomachs bloated from the cancer and our arms and legs became Halloween skeletons. We were scary.

After it was all over, I would feel foolish, stupid to end up widowed at 29; no one does that; I must have made a terrible mistake somehow. My mother certainly thought I had.

Yet a deeper knowing in me understood the lesson, even as I fought against it; so used to arguing with my wisdom, fighting with the world. Only when I was exhausted, starving, laid out by grief could I finally surrender; a surrender that came naturally to Paul. He seemed ready for whatever came next, enjoying the adventure of dying as much as he savored the thrill of being alive.

Paul appears to me now in a dream, wakes me from a deep slumber on the floor beside the bed. He's vibrantly healthy, happy and smiling, pulling me to stand up. "Wake up" he says. "Wake up and hold me like you said you would." I open my eyes and realize another day has cycled in through the window, illuminating us with rainy light, dappled and glowing. His labored breathing hasn't changed.

"Paul was just with me. He's ready to go," I say to his mother, moving to stand by the bed. She nods. We ask everyone to leave and we stand beside him, looking out the window at the soft summer rain, the green gentle foothills sloping upwards. We rub his arms and legs.

"Go play outside my baby, I'll always love you. I'll be okay. You're free to go," I whisper in his ear.

At those words, his tortured breathing stops; he takes one peaceful sigh and the light leaves his body. I watch it rise and travel up through the window and out to the green hills. We move to the window watching; the rain seems to lift briefly, then sprinkle again, sunlight peppering in through the clouds, shining in on us – a golden surprise.

This is a moment beyond words. My logical mind can't understand it. But my heart and soul know. I've just witnessed a miracle; an everyday miracle, a soul lifting peacefully from a body, slipping into the invisible. It's not a death. What a very wrong thing to call it. He shifted gracefully into something, purposefully, lovingly towards – not away from. He freed himself, leaving like a gentle kiss, slipping blissfully towards what I once called "heaven."

I feel giddy, without borders, lifted. I know in an instant that there is a rule, a law, a purpose to everything, to my life, to Paul's pain; that I've always been guided, held to the task I came here to accomplish.

This sense of knowing follows me for days and weeks. I see the divine order within each moment; signs that all is well in every conversation with a friend, in the magical apartment that Paul reveals to me in a dream and I rent the next day. I feel light and free, untethered and joyful, without appetite for food or sleep.

Living in the invisible realms now, my true home, I'm aware of the briefness of earthly lifetimes. I feel held by the angels who cherish me; they whisper in my ear at night when Paul visits, wrapping his fuzzy legs around mine in bed; holding me close until an angel calls him away.

This physical world is truly not real and it's such a relief to know it. Fully. Vividly. Through my senses know it. Costumes peel away. I see spirit everywhere. Paul has taken me with him.

Until my body pulls me back down to this weighty realm – the one I agreed to live in. But I don't want to feel this heaviness, don't want to be fully back in the body. I want my awareness to perch above it, heart soaring in the invisible. Everything I want is there not here and yet my body comes tumbling down, crashing into the earth with such force that I dry heave all night. It's been four weeks, maybe five, since Paul died.

The lack of food and sleep, the exhaustion from months of changing canisters of bile, adjusting tubes, filling syringes, measuring fluids, giving shots, counting pills, sleeping on the floor beside his bed, praying, cheering, living fearlessly in dark terror of what awaited.

Those vivid pictures of Paul's disintegration pour back into my soul now poisoning my once sweet dreams of him. I feel sick, sicker than I've ever felt. Friends grow concerned over my weight loss, take me to dinner. The smell of food sends me running outside of every café, every restaurant, every kitchen. Dry heaving in the grass. Embarrassed. Just want to go home.

Finally I eat grapes and they stay.

I need to write, to tell this story, the story of Paul. I spend hours at the typewriter filling in the details of pain. I write 90,000 words of torture. No one can read it. Too much suffering but how well I've documented it. Perhaps journalism school, they suggest. But it's what happened to Paul, I tell them. Doesn't matter. Unpublishable.

But I must tell it. Start journalism school. Get a job at the paper. Profoundly wise editor pushes me to write an article about the Boulder Hospice. I finally do. It breaks me wide open.

I move to Mexico when a girlfriend invites me to visit her.

December 1981: Mazatlan, Mexico - Eighteen months after Paul's death

Grief is my ocean warm and salty. In Mazatlan, I find the mountainous waves comforting as they grind me into the sand

and spit me out breathless on the beach. They wash me clean. I pray to the goddess of the Sea of Cortez.

Instead I meet Emilio.

"You dive with me today?" White sun-bleached hair carelessly long and scattered, framing green eyes, a rounded body, soft and smooth as a Grouper. Fascinating energy. He reeks joy. My joyful Emilio. He has never emptied a bile canister and sees me as someone who has never emptied one either. He speaks little English. I have no Spanish. I'm grateful for the lack of words. The disconnect.

I dive with him.

I love the round soft sound of his name, Emilio. Emilio. Emilio. No Edges, like his round body full as a dolphin, ancient wisdom in the eyes, soul-to-soul communication; bypass the logic brain when words fail to communicate. Go right to the heart. This is for me. All of it.

Six months later we share a tiny apartment where I learn to make eggs over easy on a fresh corn tortilla with chopped tomato and pepper salsa and refried beans.

"Tonight I'll teach you the names of the body parts," he grins. "We start with the head and move down." His English has improved quickly. His smile is a crack of light shining into my dark cave. We play and play, catching grouper each day for dinner; he spears octopus in the rocks, pulls lobsters out of hiding to make ceviche on the boat.

His neck smells like the ocean and his rough skin feels the way I imagine an elephant's trunk would feel, different from anything I've known before, thrilling. It erases me. I'm joyful to forget.

He teaches me to swim beside him, become one with the hammerheads, silently stalk the red snapper, not flap my fins against the surface as I dive down, descend quietly to the bottom and find octopus hiding in the rocks. He hands me the spear and I stab at it, black ink swirling around us, swimming up through the murky water bursting to the surface with my arm raised high: I got it! Cheers from Pedro, watching from the boat deck, arms folded, wondering about this peculiar thin and muscular American girl and when Emilio will finally leave her to go back to his sweet voluptuous wife in Mexico City.

My world rocks to the rhythm of water, slow and lazy; rising in the mornings to check the waves with Emilio; is the water clear, will it be calm enough to dive today? Nothing exists beyond this little beach town. There's nothing in the entire world except this. My money comes from teaching aerobics in town with my American girlfriend Donna who runs Los Aerobicos De Mazatlan.

Emilio's money comes from his dive business; I assist him, encouraging tourists to trust us, let us guide them into murky waters. Our uncomplicated routine reminds me of the invisible, the place I long for, completely removed from the heaviness of Boulder, Colorado and who I once was.

Standing at the bow of the boat with Emilio, our sea-bleached-hair matching strand for strand, my French creole skin now browner than his. I devote myself to this impossibly pale-skinned Aztec Indian; my green eyed blonde haired Mexican twin. I disappear gladly at his side, forgetting I once had a husband, tried to be a writer, disappointed my family.

As the boat breaks the waves, Emilio whistles to the manta rays skimming gleefully across the sea in front of us – his smiling face creased and cracked like weathered wood. "Do you have a wife Emilio?" "Yes, and a child. We are divorcing. It takes awhile to do this here. But this is not for you to worry about Sue. I am here with you." Yes, you are. And that's everything and nothing. And I'll take it.

He holds me close, so close it's hard to breathe. I love the danger, the thrill of not catching my breath, of surrendering, falling deep into the dark Sea of Cortez – a beautiful seductive lady who beckons me beneath the surface, promising death whenever I choose.

I study Spanish in El Centro at L'Escuela de Idiomas, taking the bus from our apartment in the afternoons when I'm not teaching fitness, buying papayas, mangoes, papas and aquacates para hoy at El Mercado to go with the snapper Emilio brings home for dinner.

He takes the bus with me, leaning into me in the last seat. We're silent, attuned to each other, peaceful in the crowd, enjoying the jostle of the bumpy road. In the evenings, we feast with his friends on ceviche and broiled fish; or walk the silvery beach where he finds starfish washed up in the tides and a lost baby duckling that he wraps safely inside his shirt to bring home.

We take the bus to Pollo Kawa for grilled chicken so fresh it was roaming wild behind the fire pit just hours before we eat it. Emilio knows the family and offers to help. We sit picking stones from the dried beans that will soon go on the fire to make spicy refritos for customers. I only understand pieces of their lively conversation, but I laugh and smile tirelessly. I'm sure I've never known such joy.

It's a year later, or maybe a year and a half, when Emilio asks me to help him paint the boat, and we spend the hot afternoon covering the old wooden dinghy in the hue of a cloudless summer sky. He is quiet and troubled and I know that today is the day. "Is she moving here Emilio?" "Yes, it must be this way. I will move out of our place this week." And he does.

For awhile I stay, teaching my classes, never wanting to speak English again, learning new verbs, riding the bus to El Centro for papayas, reading Hemingway late into the night, writing stories about Emilio that never quite capture his soul; can't find words to describe his fearless joy, his crushing smile, the way his sweet voice lingers deep inside me long after he's packed his diving gear and walked out the door. But the Sea of Cortez slowly slides up over the sand, floods the pockmarked streets and sweeps into my soul like a dark dank hurricane of grief. It finds me.

The last time I see Emilio, I'm riding the bus to El Centro, packed in the back of the crowd, by the window. We stop to let more people on and Emilio is standing there at the bus stop waiting for the bus that goes the other way. We see each other. I bang on the window calling his name. I can't get it to open. He spreads his arms wide with his palms to the sky, his eyes deep and sad, not saying anything, then brings his hands to his heart. He smiles. It's a terrific broad smile like I've seen lots of times before. He makes a sign with his index finger and his thumb, a little circle – like everything will be okay. He mouths the words: "See you later." The bus starts moving and I watch him standing there for as long as I can.

7

CELEBRATING WHAT?

Ten years after Emilio - Summer 1991 in Boulder Colorado

I'm not sure what to do for my 40th birthday, I say to Margaret. We're standing side by side surveying galleys that hang on the large wall in front of us; the entire September issue displayed, page-by-page. Red pen marks note mistakes to be corrected or ads to be switched.

"Hmm," she says thoughtfully. "That's a hard one. A year ago I would have said let's plan a great party with live music and dancing."

We look at each other and grin. So much time has passed in a year. Our spiritual journeys have bent time and space for both of us. While I've spent my days meditating before Babaji and hauling rocks, she has spent hers living in a spiritual community, learning a new way of eating, sleeping, and loving - down to the last kernel of food she puts in her mouth each day.

We are both transformed. Born again. Yet still standing here side-by-side cranking out this magazine to bring home our paychecks. Still single and childless. And I am soon turning 40.

"I want to do a ceremony at Shambhava retreat center for my birthday, if Babaji agrees," I explain. "I'd like to bring my friends there. It would be different. But powerful. Would you come?"

"In a heartbeat, honey, in a heartbeat," she says hugging me.

Later at the ashram, after dinner, I sit before Babaji in the sunroom, eyes closed, listening to his answers to each question the Sangha members ask. Feeling the wisdom of his words pour over me; it's like drinking sweet honey nectar, nourishing and rich.

"Babaji," I say when the room is quiet, "I'd like to celebrate my 40th birthday here with a ceremony of some kind, maybe a fire ceremony, to burn up all those parts of myself I want to release for good."

"Are you up for it Sue? A fire ceremony? Releasing your addictions? This is serious stuff. You might end up happy!" He laughs gleefully, his voice deep and kind, closing his eyes to commune with Nityananda, then opening them to smile broadly at me and nod.

The other students laugh. It feels encouraging, kindred.

After awhile, eyes closed, deeply inhaling, circulating his breath, Babaji says: "This is good, Sue. What will you burn away?"

"My small self. My fear and anger. My grief. My addiction to impossible men."

"We will have to build a very large fire," he says laughing again. "This could set the land ablaze."

Brian, sitting beside me, says, "This fire could burn down the entire world, a sort of global cleansing." This elicits heartfelt laughter from all of us, especially me. In this Sangha I feel at once accepted and criticized for my foibles and mistakes. This is where I come to confess, to lay my sins on the floor.

By now the Sangha know my tale of broken hearts, dying husbands, and married men. So it's a relief to hear this warm laughter circle us as we talk about the enormous fire we must build to burn my past away.

Faith speaks up. "It would be a great ceremony for all of us. We could chant around the fire and burn all of our negativity. That's a powerful Nityananda practice as well, to use the purification of fire."

"Yes, it's a good idea. And everyone is invited to Sue's 40th birthday fire," says Babaji, grinning at me, nodding his approval.

The plans begin.

Faith takes me aside in the dining hall and we mark the dates on her calendar. I tell her I'm inviting friends to come up and rent cabins for the weekend to join us. She's like my sister planning this, all whispers and giggles, lovely and intoxicating.

"I'll make a special dinner," she says. "Something southern for you," her blue eyes dazzling in the dim light of the dining hall, her fair skin vivid against a purple silk shawl. "And Brian can lead a meditation hike to the Buddha rocks." She smiles and makes more notes in her notebook. "This will be good for all of us, Sue. The whole Sangha will benefit."

I'm already seeing it, overwhelmed with gratitude. She stands to leave and we hug; "Thank you so much Faith," I whisper as she holds me close against her chest and her sweetness floods my senses, washing over me like a summer rain.

At work, I hand out invitations to certain friends, my staff members, some of the designers, and Margaret of course. The invitations invite them to a Friday night fire ceremony and dinner with hopes they'll rent a dorm bunk or cabin to stay for the entire weekend - complete with Saturday hike and meditation on the Buddha rocks overlooking the river.

September 1991: Turning 40 at Shambhava Mountain Retreat

It's Friday night and the dining hall is warm and smoky, wood burning stoves glowing at each end of the room, tables slowly filling with New Times friends, Sangha members, yoga students, as they arrive from evening drives up the winding steep roads that lead away from Boulder.

I sit between Faith and Margaret at the long wooden tables – eating black eyed peas with greens and honey sweet corn bread. My heart feels full and broken wide open; so many friends have driven up here, far from their comfortable lives, deep into these woods peppered with exotic golden shrines and bronzed six armed goddesses, spicy incense hanging in the air even here in the dining hall where Faith and the kitchen staff have served this delightful meal – an homage to my southern childhood.

Babaji enters with a flourish of robes and takes his place at the head of a table, surrounded by students, nodding to me, smiling, filling the room with his deep generous laugh.

My two sisters, Margaret and Faith, don't like each other, a sort of chemical aversion. To me they're both deep soul memories, old friends, yet here they guard against each other, competitive, one outdoing the other with laughter and conversation.

On one side of me, Faith outlines our weekend plans explaining it will be windy but Brian is building the bonfire in the woods beyond the cabins where there's a big sand barrier around a fire pit. "But we have to be careful," she says, "Fire hoses ready." She closes her eyes, circulates her breath, opens them to gaze at Babaji engaged in lively conversation with a student beside him. He senses it, stops talking, closes his eyes to circulate his breath, then looks directly at her, transfixed. She inhales, almost a gasp, and sighs like someone finishing a delectable meal - four courses with chocolate for dessert. He turns back to his conversation and she whispers in my ear, "We'll get started after dinner. Nityananda will be with us. And of course Babaji." She giggles, gives me a quick hug, her thick flower scented hair spilling around me.

On my other side, Margaret entertains the New Times people with spirited stories, her powerful voice pulling everyone's attention, her head thrown back in breathy laughter, dark hair pulled into a tight pony tail, spinning tales of all-night dancing parties with community friends, sharing just enough truth to keep it real and not enough sex to feed the rumor mill at New Times.

Faith hands me a pad of yellow paper. "Write down all the pieces of yourself that you want to release, burn in the fire. Fold each piece up carefully and bring them all to the fire pit. We'll start in 30 minutes." She gets up, moves gracefully to lean over and kiss Babaji's cheek. She whispers in his ear. He reaches up to kiss her mouth. The energy between them pulls everyone's focus; the room quiets. We see the thing we all long for, dazzling and extraordinary; passionate love after 20 years at each other's side.

She leaves in a sweep of blue silk and the lingering scent of rose oil.

I finish eating and hurry back to my rented cabin to write out my sins, my grievances, complaints to my higher self; impossible love, men who can't stay; I list their names, realize it's every man I know, including my father and my dead husband Paul. I add in the self-doubt, stubbornness, anger that I always bring to the table, which I no longer want, too heavy to carry; more things, my mother's disregard for who I am; no it's more, her dislike for what I am, my sense that it matters, that her love matters; no it's more, a kind of hatred she carries for who I am deep inside and how I look on the surface, the word "ugly" which she first introduced, named me at a vulnerable age; no it's more, a threat she feels around me, a fear that I see her, past her charms, her cute personality, her lovely southern voice; no it's more, that I embarrass her, that my very face, my dark eyes, my natural olive skin shames her because it IS her, her creole race mixed with ancient slave blood that she so hates, fought to bury in her past, leave behind with her professionally coiffed and colored hair, porcelain skin that never sees sunlight, to marry my freckle-skinned blue-eyed worthy Irish father.

So much is revealed in those final moments of finishing the list, running out of yellow paper, writing on toilet paper, Kleenex; would've torn up the bed sheets to color them with words but the gong bell rings outside and it's time to trek into the woods.

Stepping out of my cabin into the evening chill, I hear the chanting, pure and distinctive, voices drifting through the tall pines, wind whipping smoke into the night sky, darkening the moon. I hurry towards the sound, emerging into the yellow light of the fire, flames thin and soaring in the middle of the sand pit, thirty or forty people circling the towering bonfire that Brian built, standing, swaying, chanting Om Namah Shivaya as wind whips the smoke around the circle like a hurricane.

I join the circle and we chant into the night, wrapping wool blankets around each other, eyes tearing from the ash, Babaji's voice so deep and resonant, impossible to ignore, like a giant roto-rooter uprooting me where I stand. Time slides backwards on itself, two centuries or more of memories, old pain, heaving from my gut, rising upwards with the sacred chant, merging into the billowy smoke; images I no longer want - shame and disappointment at myself, at the hurt I chose to feel, the hurt I caused others, the pitifulness of me, poor me, whom I didn't have to be, no longer would be.

Circling the fire now, wind whipping my ponytail sharp and painful against my cheeks, eyes stinging; a sudden gust seeming to lift me from my feet as I toss the yellow papers one by one into the crimson flames and everyone carries the chant up and away into the dark sky. Brian heaves a pine branch on top of the pile and gray smoke rises, clouding everything and everyone, filling my lungs and heart until the cold wind sweeps in, purging the air around us; we sing long into the moonless night.

Later in the weekend, after morning meditation, Brian leads us on an hour-long hike to the top of the Buddha rocks, a pinnacle of granite towering above a steep valley where a lonely river twists and turns below; three golden Buddhas have been hand-painted on the tall granite slabs leading to the summit – a near perfectly flat resting place, an array of boulders forming a kind of sitting area high above the breezy sweep of the narrow canyon.

We gather on top of these granite boulders and Brian explains that to meditate in beauty we must be open to receive the gift of nature's splendor without being distracted, to tune inwards no matter the activities of the outer world. He rings a gong and we begin, sunlight warming our skin against the cold rock, trying to keep eyes closed amidst the beauty of towering evergreens, shimmering silver granite and the call of ravens flying high and fast around us.

A few minutes in, a large black raven perches in front of me, only feet away, disturbing the air around my face. I think I'm dreaming, but I'm awake; the rock cold and hard against my butt. It's impossible to ignore the raven. He stares at me, fearless, thoughtful, then singing, urgent and endless; a song of discontent turning into a warning or maybe a guide, instructions from beyond, the story he tells rising in pitch and frequency; you must hear me, you must listen, you need to do this, you have to, you need to, you have to...

He goes on and on, I hear people beside me moving, making sounds, gasps, some of them backing away from the bird. I sit mesmerized, listening to every word, our eyes locked, until it begins to snow, the sun long gone behind dark clouds, large white flakes floating gently, covering the silvery rocks, evergreen trees, our bare heads now blanketed in snow as I watch the great black raven turn and opening his magnificent wings, take flight, disappearing downwind into the white beauty of the canyon far below.

Brian rings the gong and stands up. We straighten our cold legs and lean into each other to rise. Someone begins to speak, others giggle. I hear someone whisper "Incredible," - but Brian hushes us and we follow him in silence down slippery, now icy wet rocks to get to the cover of the trees, the tall pines where we follow the long and winding trail back to the dining hall.

Later emerging from the snowy trees into the clearing that wraps around the dining hall, we realize it's warm and summery here, the sun suddenly hot on our wet clothes. Every season has poured itself upon us within the past hour and it exhilarates us.

Over lunch, Babaji listens to our animated stories, the impossible raven, his relentless singing, the sudden snow, the dramatic weather, what does it mean, how could it be real? He listens, closing his eyes in meditation, breathing in deeply and holding it. A long exhale as we all become silent, watching him, careful, poised. And then he laughs, deep and melodious; it echoes, bouncing off the high wooden beamed ceilings, pulling the attention of everyone eating at the tables. The room quiets.

"Life ain't easy for a girl named Sue," he says softly. Then turning towards me: "I don't know what it means. But you do. It was your message and your soul knows. Your soul ALWAYS knows." And looking almost angry, annoyed with me for asking, he rises, lingering scent of frankincense in the air as he stands, wrapping his voluminous orange silk robes around him, suddenly pressing his gigantic open hand into the table, pausing to circulate his breath, then swatting the top of my head, his enormous fingers reaching down to cover my scalp, my hair, holding it there for a second; breath knocked out of me, almost falling backwards, the room spinning, a pure powerful force burning from the top of my head down my spine, spinning out through my toes, like a lightning strike. I feel raw and opened up, cleansed like only fire can cleanse, like I don't remember who was wearing my clothes a minute ago, who got dressed in them that morning. I watch him leave the room, and he's my father, my dead husband Paul, my married lover Christopher, Emilio and my mother. I cry with heart ripping sobbing grief, impossible to explain, head down on the table, gasping. "Let it go honey, let it all go," whispers Margaret beside me, rubbing my back in circles, leaning into me, sobbing against my shoulders, her own demons pouring out onto the table, tears blending with mine on the dark wood. The fire ceremony has done its job.

8

COMING HOME

July 1981 – Mobile Alabama

My dad calls, asks me to fly home. It's been a year since Paul died and I haven't been back to Alabama since we met. Most of my family had flown to Colorado the year before for our wedding, hippie style, at a tiny church up Four Mile Canyon, with a potluck reception at our cabin down the road, against the creek, where the water bubbled so loudly the sound filled our bedroom at night. Heavenly, like sleeping under a waterfall, Paul said. What I've always wanted, I said. Mom said nothing, standing in the middle of the living room, arms crossed, lips pursed.

My dress was simple; long pale satin with a blue ribbon at the waist, made by a friend. I carried gardenias, felt divine, marinated in love. Exquisite, said Paul. Mom said nothing, sitting in the front row next to dad, looking down, her hands nervously twisting in her lap.

During the potluck reception at our cabin, dad explores our bedroom loft asking questions about the photos on the wall: Is that you on top of that mountain Sue? Yes dad. Paul and I climbed it awhile ago. And those people you're with? My students from

Outward Bound School. I was their mountaineering instructor, we'd just finished a three-week course in the Maroon Bells. You look so happy Sue. I was dad. I am.

He smiles, delighted by the pictures, the loft, the sound of the creek, shaking his head and nodding; this man who loves simple, who loves oceans, feeling right at home.

When Paul was dying in our living room, my family couldn't come to help. So many reasons, said mom. So far away. Alabama. Colorado. Different worlds. Your sister's only 21, too young, don't want her to see that kind of thing. Of course mom, I understand. I'm 28.

Paul's funeral had been a potluck with climbing friends, memories shared under a glorious starry night with a slip of a moon. Impossible to make it, said my mom. But I need to come home to see my family, I cried to her on the phone, weak like a child, needy. No, she says. Not now. I've just put a new floor in the kitchen and the dining room table is being replaced; and you know how you are, Sue Ellen, forgetting to take your shoes off at the door, not a good time, she explains.

Now, a year later, my grief gathering strength, pain going deeper inside, but looking better on the outside, eating again, teaching fitness, in journalism school, writing well, and dad calls. I want to see you, he says. Don't worry about your mother. I'll send you money for a ticket home. I'll meet you at the airport. I'm renting a little beach house for us for the week. If anybody wants to join us they can, if not, it's fine, he explains. It'll be just us. I agree, dad, great really, so happy to get to see you again.

I fly home, broken like a wreck, but much stronger than the year before. Our beach house is small, old, falling apart and perfect, just yards from the surf. Dad docks his fishing boat in the harbor down the road and in the morning we get up early; I make eggs, toast and coffee while he gathers fishing rods and tackle, the shiny red and blue feathered lures that resemble earrings, dangling and seductive. We pack sandwiches and drinks for the cooler and haul it to the car as the sun comes up; driving to the harbor studying clouds and waves, how will it be in the bay today, or should we try Sand Island, there's always trout on the north side there.

The boat is small but strong and dad steers it directly into the waves. We round Fort Morgan Point and make the choppy trek to Sand Island, waves pounding the boat up and down as we cross the wide murky mouth of Mobile Bay. I hang on to the bow rope, salt spray in my eyes, riding the waves with knees and arms bent, thrilled; looking back at dad who grins and points out a dolphin breaking the surface not far ahead of us, and then a school of them, five or six, rising up grey and sleek through the waves to glide beside our boat, their eyes watchful and kind.

We anchor in the shallows to the north of the island, in the calmer water. He wants to pull the net, find baitfish in the shallows. We get the bulky seine out from under the bow and jump in; each of us holding a tall pole attached to opposite ends of it. We drag it through the low waves, side-by-side, in sync with each other, trying to be silent, watching crabs and stingrays take off in front of us. I try not to be afraid of the rays. But I am afraid of the Bull Shark that shows its fin a few yards ahead. I look over at dad; it's nothing, he nods, don't worry. He motions to keep moving forward. I put my focus on holding the pole upright and dragging the net just as he does, exactly as he does. He's taller than me, maybe 6′2″ to my 5′7″; he can push through the currents with no trouble. I try not to lose my balance, stay parallel to him, keep up, pretend it's easy. We pull in tiny jumping minnows, a few crabs, a flounder, some shrimp and catfish. We use it to bait our rods and cast for trout. Later we sit in the boat eating cold cheese sandwiches, drinking ginger ale and Barq's root beer. The day has warmed, my head pounds from the sun; he wants to get moving, feel a breeze, so we troll the calm side of the island, poles jutting up from either corner of the boat, motor running slow, lines dragging in the murky water, snagging fish as my sister calls it. We catch mackerel for dinner.

At night on the deck we clean the fish. He teaches me to make a precise cut, perfect filets in one slice. I practice until I'm good at this. He likes to broil them with a little butter. I make salad and warm the French bread. Afterwards we sit on the deck watching the night sky, him smoking his pipe, the cherry wood scent rising sweet and sharp around us. It's the same pipe I bought him years ago to get him to stop smoking cigarettes. I bring him coffee to go with his smoke. We are happy just looking at stars, pointing out constellations; I tell him stories about my mountain climbing days in Colorado and how at night I could watch Orion rise in the eastern sky and tell the time by where the moon was. He loves these stories.

He tells me stories about growing up in New Orleans, Algiers – where he knew everyone, played baseball, had so many friends at his Catholic school, loved his family; the great house on the corner always filled with people, parties and laughter; his father running the ferry across the muddy Mississippi, wealthy and powerful. It couldn't have been better he says, eyes moist. I know. I say. I love those stories.

"Dad, why did you move us here? To Alabama?"

A long pause while he puffs thoughtfully on the spicy tobacco, legs crossed gracefully, looking up at the stars, his once dark hair now peppered with silver. "A lot of reasons, a hard decision," he says slowly. "Your mother didn't get along with Grandpa. She thought it would be better for us to get away from my family, from both of our families," he looks over at me, his pale eyes clear and kind, "You know she was ashamed of some of her people. I thought maybe we'd be happier here. Mobile had a lot of new industry with the paper mills, and it seemed like a good place for my engineering career. And look at this beauty," he extends his long arm out towards the sea in front of us, waves slipping back and forth like milky foam in the moonlight, white sand shimmering like the stars above. "I love this," he says, peacefully puffing on the cherry smoke.

"I hated Mobile," I say, sipping the hot coffee, "it was nothing after New Orleans." But I understand how my dad, the peacekeeper, would have thought it through that way. "I know you did," says dad. "And your mother was unhappy here. You know she loves you Sue, she does. She just can't show it."

Days go by in this simple rhythm, rising early to fish, talking late into the night under the stars, happily catering to my dad; making simple dinners that delight him, sharing our favorite climbing and nautical knots; mine are the bowline and figure eight, his are the cleat hitch and the sheet bend. We delight each other. He's a best friend; no, he's Paul, when he looks up at me suddenly on the boat and his blue eyes are the color of the sea and his smile so wide I feel wrapped in love; we are perfectly suited for each other. But he is my father, not my lover, not my husband, not mine. And this is all pretend, a week of something I'll never have again.

My younger sister Ann drops in to visit for a day, studying for college exams, and then my brother Micky for an afternoon, not studying for his; and then Roy, just back from law school, bringing more fishing rods and taking dad off in the boat without me; our peaceful routine slips away. I'm the big sister again, worried about keeping the house clean so we can get our deposit back, please don't make a mess. I'm stressed until they leave.

My dearest childhood girlfriend Crissie calls the beach house, tells me she's home visiting her parents in Mobile. She lives in California now. Her dad has a fishing boat and their beach house is just across the bay. Can we spend the day together, I plead.

Three months after Paul died, Crissie had come to visit me in Boulder. We'd gone skiing. Our trip ended with her taking a bad fall that bruised her leg, looked so weird, too many colors for a bruise. But we laughed it off and she got on the flight back to Berkeley. When the plane landed, her body had painted itself in purple bruises, head to toe. They took her by ambulance to the hospital where they diagnosed leukemia. The bad kind. She called to tell me this and I hung up wanting to die. Not Paul. Not Crissie. Take me. Please…

But she'd gone to Seattle and had the bone marrow transplant to save her life and was doing quite well she said. Sure she'd visit us. Her dad would drop her off at the harbor and my dad would take us fishing at Sand Island. We agreed. It was our childhood stomping grounds after all.

On the day of her visit, while my dad casts for speckled trout, Crissie and I walk the perimeter of Sand Island. She wears a scarf around her head, not much hair grown back in yet. The day is hot, too bright, no trees, sun pounding on our heads. We run through the shallow pools to cool ourselves, avoiding the stingrays and crabs; shrieking and giggling when we see the distant fin of a Bull Shark.

She tells me stories of suffering that are so similar to Paul's, so familiar and painful; she'll never have children now, she explains, choking on the words. "What's the hardest part?" I ask. "My dad," she says, starting to cry, "He wants me to live so badly." We stand in the low surf holding each other, crying about our dads who love us too much, too much to take in all of this suffering. She feels fragile in my arms, tiny, no longer the powerful girl I remember.

We say good-bye at the harbor. She stands beside her dad on his impressive double deck fishing boat complete with young handsome fishing guide, whom Crissie pretends to flirt with. They wave down to us standing side-by-side on the dock as they pull away. My father and I wave back until we can no longer see their boat on the horizon. When we turn away, my insides are churning, I feel nauseous, trying not to cry, don't want to upset my dad. "She looks pretty good," says dad, his lips tight, clearing his throat, not looking at me. "I don't think so," I say. "I don't think I'll ever see her again, dad. It's something I just know." We are quiet and sullen on the short drive back to the beach house; dad clearing his throat too many times, looking over at me briefly, his eyes moist and pained, neither of us speaking.

She's gone in three months. It is the last time I see my friend.

By the fifth day at the beach, dad is feeling guilty that he left mom in the city, made a decision against her will, saw the disowned daughter, the black sheep. We catch a dozen mackerel and meticulously filet them. Dad places them in foil and wraps them carefully in ice inside the cooler. He wants to take them home to cook in mom's kitchen and have a family dinner. With mom. His kind spirit won't allow him to continue his act of willful disobedience. He imagines she'll be glad to see us, happy to eat the fish dinner. I know it won't go this way, I tell him. I know the story, have seen it too often, but I go along, hopeful.

We drive into Mobile and he stops at the grocery store to get more things for our fish dinner. He calls mom from the payphone, walks back to the car with his head hanging, his lips a thin line across his perfectly chiseled features, blue eyes dim and cloudy.

"She doesn't want us bringing over the fish, says it will be messy and we'll have the fishing gear to clean. She just doesn't want the mess in her house on her new floor," he says, trying to sound logical. "We'll go to Roy's house and cook it there. Micky and Ann will join us." They do.

It's a sad dinner; Mom calling the house ten or twenty times yelling at dad about his many transgressions; bringing me home against her will, renting a beach house, trying to bring the fishing mess to her house. He listens, nods, keeps picking up the phone, coming back to the table, calm and quiet. Roy picks up one of the calls and yells at mom. Tells her she's insane.

"This is why I left," I say, putting my head down on the table. Can't eat the fish, push it around with my fork, the old grief nausea returning.

I fly back to Boulder the next day never seeing the mom who really loves me but just can't show it.

Fall 1991 – Shambhava Retreat Center, Rollinsville, Colorado

With each passing week, I fall more deeply in love with the chilly pre-dawn meditations, incense filling my groggy senses; our voices harmonizing as the sun rises through the windows, rhythmic chanting of the Sanskrit words comforting my busy mind that somewhere halfway though the hour floats up through the top of my head to dance with Lakshmi, Ganesha, and Nityananda - leaving me joyful.

Walking through early morning snow as the bell summons us to breakfast, sun low in the eastern sky, diamond shards of light skimming across the meadow on the trail to the dining hall; my heart soars with the powerful sounds of the devotional Guru Gita echoing within and I sing the Sanskrit words to myself:

Gurur buddhyaa tmano naanyat satyam satyam na samshayah,

Tallaa bhaartham prayat nastu kartavyo manee shibhih

Later learning their meanings:

"The Guru is not different from the conscious self. Without doubt, this is the truth, this is the truth. Therefore wise men should make an effort to seek him."

"To him nothing is insentient, the whole world is filled with Consciousness; joined with the Eternal, having passed beyond the gunas (physical) - To that Nityananda, I bow."

And later in the text: "Reciting the Guru Gita always bestows peace in all respects, grants a good son to a barren woman, averts women's widowhood and always brings good fortune."

In Sanskrit the words feel transformative.

Getting to know my fellow meditators, lawyers, veterinarians, teachers, students, musicians; hearing their stories and losses, their understanding of this work, as we fold laundry, wash dishes, sweep floors. I love it most when Babaji sits in the sunroom after meals answering questions, laughing at our foibles, spreading his warm energy through the room - brighter than the high-altitude sun that shines through the window setting his crimson robes ablaze with light.

I crave the peacefulness of cleaning cold and empty guest cabins, learning to perfect hospital corners with the bed sheets, inspect the polished wooden floors and gleaming white toilets afterwards as if Nityananda himself were planning to stay there. All of this work opens my heart in ways that trickle down to my small apartment in Boulder - now decorated with bronzed deities, sacred Tangka paintings, and sandalwood incense burners. On work days, I rise early enough to chant the full 60 minute Guru Gita, sitting cross-legged on my meditation cushion facing Nityananda's picture on the wall, holding my hand in front of my heart; fill me with love Nityananda, nourish me, guide me through this work day.

He walks through my rooms. I'm never alone. He visits my dreams, pats my head, sends Shakti down through my toes; I recognize his large hands and the sudden breath that wakes me up. I'm walking in the ordinary world while plugged into the extraordinary. Thank you Babaji. Thank you Faith. Thank you Nityananda. At work, I take twenty minutes each afternoon to shut my office door, close my eyes and repeat mantra; mala prayer beads running through my fingers.

One weekend, Babaji has a special visitor, a somewhat famous Yogi, whom he invites to come up and teach. This teacher brings his full Sangha, over 100 members. They fill our cabins and we move extra tables into the dining hall. The ashram buzzes with new energy. Faith asks me to help in the kitchen.

"We'll need lots of Spanakopita for the weekend," she explains, teaching me to gently fold the delicate layers of Phyllo dough around the chopped, spiced spinach and cheese mixture.

"How did you meet Babaji?" I ask as she adjusts knobs and temperatures on the large commercial gas stove, then bends down to peer into the oven, one finger poking a spanakopita, testing it for crispness, steam rising to ruffle her wavy dark hair gathered loosely around her head into a top knot, a halo of soft curls escaping around her forehead.

"My father was killed in a car accident when I was 13. I was devastated. I was the oldest girl of nine kids, mom worked full time, we were pretty poor," she smiles as she tells me this, grabbing a wooden spoon to blend cinnamon, cloves and ginger into a hefty pot of honey-sweet tea and milk. "It was up to me to make dinner, get the kids to do their homework, keep everything running. But I wanted to do it; my mom was struggling." She grabs a cup from the shelf, dips it quickly into the steamy pot, sips the chai, closes her eyes and smiles; then adds another dollop of cloves into the brew.

She tells her painful childhood story with such ease but I know there was more to it than that; Faith, always graceful, choosing to only tell it that way, or only see it that way. "What about you?" she asks, turning to face me, smile widening. "Tell me more about your childhood, your dad, I know you loved him a lot, and your siblings."

By now I'm so familiar with her quick re-directs; the way she dislikes the personal reveal, hastens to put the lens on someone else to protect herself, or Babaji, I'm not sure which.

I laugh, helping her pour the hot chai into pitchers for the dining hall. "Faith, you know my story. I've told it often enough, dysfunctional, funny southern family, you know the rest," I grin looking at her across the steaming chai. "Your turn," I say and she laughs out loud, eyes looking into mine, perhaps wondering how deeply she can trust me. Then fixing a stray Bobbi pin on her topknot she pauses, circulating her breath, eyes closed, hesitating.

"I left home pretty young, around the time I was 16. For awhile I was involved with the wrong crowd, sort of a punk. I was lost, looking for answers about why my dad died and where he'd gone. The Catholic Church didn't ring true for me anymore," she says without looking at me, focused on a fresh tray of spanakopita.

"After awhile I started reading books about eastern traditions, like Buddhism. A girlfriend told me about Swami Rudrananda who was giving a talk at the East West Center in Boston, not too far from where I lived. We went to see him," she looks up at me, a huge smile across her face. "He was a Jewish Swami from Brooklyn," she laughs, shaking her head at the memory. "A funny looking bald guy with bushy eyebrows and the kindest, softest brown eyes. He owned a couple antique stores in New York."

She pauses, inhales, circulating her breath. "Rudi was love, pure love. He blessed everyone who knew him." She says it quietly, thoughtfully, as she busies herself again, chopping onions for Aloo Gobi. I notice her eyes are moist, maybe from the onions.

"Were you sort of in love with Rudi?" I ask in a whisper, standing close beside her to peel the un-chopped onions; both of us aware of the sound of the back door opening, distant voices in the laundry room.

"A little bit," she smiles, without looking at me. "The way it is with teachers."

"The way I'm a little bit in love with Babaji? The way all the women here are a little bit in love with Babaji?" I ask, laughing softly beside her. She looks directly at me; something sweet, almost grateful, in her eyes.

"Did you meet Babaji at Rudi's ashram?" I ask.

"Yes, he was called Jim then and he was one of the other students there, a very serious student of Rudi's work – like I was. He was a big guy always sitting at Rudi's feet, having huge Kriyas from the meditations, writhing and falling over," she laughs at the memory, briefly wiping her eyes along the edge of her apron. "But we didn't really talk then. We were both such serious students. And we both loved Rudi." She turns to unwrap more phyllo dough and looks up briefly at the picture of Rudi hanging above the counter, a large bald man with a broad smile looking down at us, amusement in his eyes.

"Tell me more about Rudi," I say, not wanting her to finish the story.

"Oh Rudi was such a good businessman, so successful. All those wealthy New Yorkers loved his imported antiques," turning to face me, leaning against the counter, looking off into the distance for a moment quiet, then, "He specialized in sacred art, deities, statues from India, China, Nepal; we really loved helping out in his store." She laughs then, her eyes bright and youthful, her face alive, before she turns back to the cutting board.

I imagine Faith and Babaji sitting at Rudi's feet in the ashram; beautiful olive-skinned dark-eyed young Babaji, curly black hair cut short around his head, tall and still beside Faith with her translucent skin, thick wavy hair, startling blue eyes; hanging out together in Rudi's store amongst the bronzed deities and imported antiques.

"Wow, I can see it," I giggle, "I bet you two were an impressive couple."

She stops chopping, turns to face me. "No," she says quickly. "Jim was married to someone else." There's a long pause and my heart skips a beat. Could it be that Faith once loved an impossible man, and yet it turned out to be possible?

She looks at me, her eyes deep and still, "We didn't get involved for a long time, a very long time. We just studied with Rudi; we were both devastated by Rudi's death - heartbroken."

I hold her gaze and nod slowly, remembering this part of the story, how Rudi died suddenly in a small plane crash in the mountains of upstate New York.

Background voices getting louder now, footsteps moving towards the kitchen until Brian bursts through the swinging doors and moves across the kitchen to rub his hands together over the stove. He nods at me, smiling, then turns to Faith; "Babaji wants you to come up to the house whenever you can," he says, pouring himself a cup of warm Chai. Faith, looking slightly relieved, wipes her hands on her apron, hangs it on a hook beside the stove, and briefly hugging me, gives instructions for the spanakopita and hurries out the door.

But I know most of the rest; how Babaji traveled to India to study with Guru Muktananda and become an initiated Swami; how he met Brian in India at Muktananda's ashram; and how Babaji was ultimately overlooked as successor to the lineage when Muktananda chose Guru Mai to continue his work, and how, somewhat later, Babaji, Faith, Brian and many of Rudi's followers moved to Colorado to start businesses in Boulder - while they continued their spiritual work, calling themselves renegade yogis. Their bakery and restaurant, now well known in Boulder, quickly became so successful that they were able to buy this land, build this ashram, and become who they are. It's part of what I love about them; how they're savvy in both worlds - the divine and the mundane.

What I don't know, and never really find out, is how their love story unfolded, if there were moments of indiscretion, unfaithfulness, impossible longing that when held up into the light of spiritual practice, of Nityananda's grace, became possible. I want to imagine this is probably true, that it did unfold in a messy way; and somehow that thought comforts me as I drive down the twisting canyon road back to my lonely apartment that still seems as if it waits for Christopher to arrive and fill the rooms with light.

Winter Expo 1992
Breckenridge, Colorado

I look down at my skis swinging back and forth below the chair lift, feels good on my back to let them swing as the chair grinds slowly up the mountain. Gordon points to someone beneath us on the slopes and we watch his young girlfriend Marion, once a competitive skier and ski instructor, weave through a crowd of skiers near the top then take off in a blur of jumps and turns beneath us, speeding down the slope. "Wow," I say to Gordon. "She's amazing." He laughs and nods.

"You seem happy Gordon. I'm glad."

We lean over the bar to watch other skiers; Gordon waves at the president of an international juice company racing a vitamin retailer. This annual Ski Expo created by Gordon is our favorite event of the year; a weekend of networking where business owners get wild, step out of their comfort zone, conduct business on mountain summits, inside cozy ski chalets, aloft on chair lifts. This year it's more popular than ever and we've jammed the Breckenridge hotels with attendees.

Gordon hands me a bar of something chocolate-looking. "This is made by my friend Ted from Nature's Bars. Try it," I bite in; it's almost good but not really. "It's terrible, right?" he says grinning. "I've told him it still needs work." He leans over the railing to yell at someone sprawled on the snow, skis scattered, poles, hats and gloves missing; "Havin a rough day, Jim?" he laughs. Jim waves at us, struggling to sit up, find his skis. "Some of these people have rarely ever skied before," Gordon says. "We should spend more time with the beginners, thank them for coming, keep them on the easy slopes."

"I'm doing as much of that as I can. Every now and then I need to take off just to feel the wind in my hair," I say.

He nods at me: "How are things in the office?" he asks as we near the top.

"Different from when you were around. Very political, lots of power games." Now we're at the top, lifting the bar, moving to the edges of the seat, poles ready.

"Okay, we'll talk soon," he says pushing off and down the slope to catch his girlfriend.

I'm happy to ski alone, take a moment to soak in the view; the wind whipped peaks; the exploding light; the high lonely basins to the left. Somewhere over there is *that* lake, highest one in the tundra, above 10,000 feet where I scattered Paul's ashes more than ten years ago on a hot July day when I could only eat grapes. I couldn't have imagined then that I'd be here now; a successful magazine editor, finally a published writer, a spiritual student of Babaji's. Yet I'm still alone. Stronger. Happier. But still single and childless.

I dig my poles into the snow and shove off, slicing easy curves down the hill, letting the speed pull me forward, loving the cold against my cheeks, the way the trees rush by in a dim blur; my mind focusing only on the next turn, the rhythm of bliss, the serenity of gravity.

I hear my name called and slow to see that it's Margaret. She introduces me to the owner of an organic whole-wheat pasta company. We make small talk and ski gently side-by-side the rest of the way down. At the bottom, we shake hands in agreement about the size of the ad he'll place in our next issue.

After a dinner networking event at the lodge, Gordon invites several of us to drop by his private condo, decorated like a pink and blue Key West cottage. When I arrive it's noisy with people, mostly folks I know. We spill into the large hot tub and across his sprawling sofa to talk business; everyone loose and lazy from the long day skiing; Gordon corners us with questions; wants to hear profit margins, sales quotas. I pretend to listen but the numbers blur into lovely hexagon-shaped snowflakes gathering one-by-one against the windowsill.

When Gordon asks me about the magazine, I find my voice; ask a business owner how he got into the natural foods world, why he started his company; that's what our readers like to know, I say, the personal side of things. This conversation wakes us up a bit; we lean in closer to hear each other's stories; a mother dying of cancer who inspires her son to seek answers outside of conventional medicine, to launch a vitamin company and later a million dollar organic food business; all their stories born of personal loss and disillusionment with a food system grown toxic or a medical paradigm unable to find a cure.

I'm charged up and fully awake now as we share these losses; feeling connected in ways I seldom do elsewhere. The room grows sweeter with each story, the light from the fireplace crimson against our faces. An herbal company owner tells us he sees his departed mom occasionally in the warehouse where they store products. We get goose bumps as he describes how young and happy she looks, nodding at him from behind a shelf. We learn that Marion, Gordon's girlfriend, lost her father and brother when she was very young and that these early losses fueled her desire to live on the edge, ski professionally, and that yes her brother checks in with her often. We hold hands like best friends.

These people are all like me inside their business suits, behind their number crunching, in spite of their warehouses and bank accounts; we are all the same beneath our skin; we are wounded healers who once held lovers and mothers in our arms, believed in happy endings, thought good people shouldn't suffer; trusted what the docs said, cleaned up blood and bile, were lifted briefly into a happy dimension to visit husbands, brothers, fathers, mothers and wives; and here we landed broken and disappointed, looking for a better way; delighted when spirits arrived unannounced in our dreams or behind the shelves of a warehouse. We formulated vitamins, crafted tinctures, grew things without chemicals, forged magazines, all to honor them, to save them; to save ourselves. I love these people, this is my family of origin. I want the evening to last forever - until it's over and we walk crunchy and tired to our rooms; laughing and hugging on the sidewalks.

The next day Gordon tells me that Christopher is arriving. "Just wanted you to know. Be careful," he says sweetly as we wait in line for the chair lift. That evening I'm not invited to Gordon's condo for the after-party; I'm pretty sure that Christopher is there. I feel outcast, separated from, excluded; somehow at fault. What a mess I've made of things.

The next day I'm sitting alone in a booth at the lodge, warming up with a cup of tea, waiting for Margaret to join me, and Christopher sits down across from me, thick layers of ski wool still on, peeling off his hat, goggles, laying them on the table, not saying anything.

We stare at each other. After awhile he says simply: "Sue."

I'm suddenly winded, unable to catch my breath. How is it possible, realistically humanly feasible, to shred the energy of a room, pierce through stillness like a machete, remove oxygen from a bustling restaurant, dazzle when everyone else is muddled; how exactly do you arrive like an apostle of light, a gospel of John, so casually and easily slide into a booth and change the air, in spite of your mortal sins, your need for penance, how do you change everything; or maybe it's just that my eyes aren't blue and yours are and that is always eternally shocking to me.

He says it again; "Sue," then, "I've only got a minute to talk, but I want to know how you are."

I look away, feeling like this is bullshit; that he already knows the answer. A painfully slow silence spreads out between us. After awhile I look back at him and say – "Why?"

He squirms in his seat, uncomfortable. I'm grateful for the noise around us, the mess and tangle of his ski clothes, his hair still matted from the wool cap, face red from the cold air, disheveled. I think he's going to rise, leave, then he leans into the back of his seat.

"Because I love you, couldn't help it. It was unavoidable; like a train wreck. I'm sorry." He looks down and I wonder for a moment if he's sad. "Then he looks up at me, sincere, thoughtful: "Do you think for a minute I don't miss you?"

I feel the train wreck, feel it in my chest, a slowly arriving sense of doom; twisted metal and mangled cars crashing against my ribs, broken bodies bobbing through my arteries, a locomotive exploding inside my stomach. I gather my things and try to stand up. I can only move in slow motion.

"Wait," he says reaching out to touch my hand. "I love you. It's just not meant to be - for now."

I pull my hand away: "I'm glad you're back with your family, happy. But you don't understand how you've hurt me."

"I do Sue, I do."

Then looking at him, "Did I love you too much? I need to know."

He looks away thoughtful, sad, then back to me: "Yes. You loved me too much. And you needed me too much." This is not a lie. This is true. And he says it sweetly, his face angelically kind, his eyes deep pools.

Why is it so hard to stand up, force my legs to move; pins and needles painful, but finally I'm up and teetering beside the booth. He stands, wraps his huge body around me - a warm bear hug; but it feels like the weight of a Water Oak or a ferry boat landing on my head, crushing me with such force that everything I know to be true gets jumbled up, swept away; drains out, all the juice, the life force, the Shakti that Babaji has given me, all flooding away, leaking out of my toes and down through the floor boards.

"You're strong Sue," he whispers in my ear. "You'll be fine, happy and in love someday soon. I know you will."

These words are it, aren't they? The final obituary, the allergic bee sting, the kinds of things doctors say when they have no hope, realize it's terminal and hand you a band-aid. And where have I heard this before, this exact phrase; yes of course it was Paul, in the final hours, the way he pointed his finger at me from a hospital bed and said don't waste your life grieving for me, get married, have babies; and voila here I am ten years later hanging on to a dead man, a stunning success of a woman, living alone without children at 40, an utterly pitiful failure; couldn't even fulfill Paul's dying wish.

Someone calls out Christopher's name from across the crowded room and he releases me, one long look into my eyes and he's off to see his friend. I feel limp and empty, my muscles turned to mush; moving towards the bathroom like I'm trying to run through an ocean, can't move forward, just can't make it, so exhausting to keep trying and finally I'm in the bathroom stall crying it out; telling Paul how sorry I am to have disappointed him so much; his ashes resting just over the hill where I'm sure he can see me here, a sorry broken piece of myself; and if Nityananda loves me at all why doesn't he just pound me on the head and erase me.

It's not until later when I'm speeding down a steep slope by myself, the wind fierce and painful on my face, that things begin to clear; tears becoming tiny specks of glistening ice and I surrender to the abyss where Christopher awaits; his golden hair lighting up the night. I take his hand and we float into the Never Land clouds, flying high above the hidden lake that hangs from a mountaintop where Paul's ashes swim inside of tiny fish and everything is perfect.

PART TWO:
THE HURRICANE

9

Three Summers of Revolution

June 1970 – Somewhere between Missouri and California

"I think I'm going to puke," I say to Chuck sitting beside me on the floor of the van. The road is bumpy, rattling, jostling us side to side; the air is heavy with marijuana and Pink Floyd wailing from the speakers.

Lotus's lean on each other in yearning
Over the hills a swallow is resting
Set the controls for the heart of the sun

"I can't find my purse, I have to find it," I mumble, digging around beneath blankets, pillows, an army salvaged back pack of Lou's and there it is, my well-worn brown suede sack with long suede pull ties around its narrow neck; the same purse I bought one year ago exactly, with Crissie, on a different adventure to California in the summer of 1969.

I put the purse in my lap; it feels empty, there's no money inside. But I have a brush, maybe a pencil, a small notebook, mirror, some lipstick my college room mate Marty, gave me before we left, and a white rosary from my grandmother, her gift for my Holy Confirmation.

"Do you know what time it is?" I ask Chuck, his dark curly hair mostly covering his half closed eyes, red-rimmed and vacant, as he turns to look at me, handing the small glowing reefer to Walter, his voice kind and deep: "It's okay," he says wrapping his arm around me. "We'll be there soon. Just be here now," he grins - pointing to the tattered blue book on the floor beside us: *Be Here Now* by Ram Dass.

But I'm not sure where *here* is.

Later, turning in to another camp ground, stumbling out of the van, Lou's laughter, Walter coughing in the distance, Chuck stands still looking up at the moon, arms outstretched; his wild hair silhouetted in the dim light. I stand beside him, our feet shoeless on the gravelly dirt, RVs humming peacefully around us, tents lit from within, scattered along the dusty road. I know we're somewhere on the way to California, but I don't know where. *Set the controls for the heart of the sun…*

Feeling hungry and sick at the same time, I find the campground bathroom and survey my dusty bell-bottomed jeans, ragged at the edges, that I bought the day I first arrived on campus just a little over a year ago; the stained white peasant blouse with dark blue smocking around the neck that I found at a Salvation Army store the day before we left Missouri for our California Dreamin' pilgrimage.

Standing at the sink, feeling disgusted with how I look and who I've become, I turn on the faucet, filling my hands with the clear cold water, splashing it on my face, my hair, beginning to cry; appalled that I'm so dirty, aware that other women are moving through the bathroom quietly, looking away as soon as their eyes land on me, filthy and crying at the sink.

Slowly I notice a lady about my mom's age standing beside me. Her hair is short and neatly styled, hair-sprayed and teased; she wears a clean floral polyester blouse and brown knit pants with little beige pumps – so similar to something my mom would wear. She hands me some paper towels, "You're hungry," she says kindly. "You'll feel better if you eat. I'll bring over some canned food for you and your friends. My daughter is gone too, somewhere out west. She's about your age. I never hear from her," She opens her purse and pulls out a twenty dollar bill, quickly folds it into the palm of my hand. "I like to help the kids we see on the road, hoping that somewhere someone feeds my daughter." She gives me a quick hug; I try not to sob while she holds me, nodding gratefully towards her as she disappears out the door.

"Here have these cans of beef stew, this bag of chips, some Tang," the lady from the restroom says emptying a bag of goodies on the dusty ground in front of us. I look up at her, wanting to climb into their humming RV and drive away with her and her husband, a large bellied man who seldom leaves the camper; how I long to escape far from here, from Lou, Walter, Frank and Chuck. The only other woman who started this trip with us, Jan, baled days ago to hitchhike home by herself. I've stayed because of a dream to live in California with Chuck, find a simple job; be happy in a warm place filled with people like me, like us.

We hurriedly open the cans of beef stew and Lou heats them over the camp stove - in between puffs on his reefer. "Tell me again why Sue doesn't smoke with us," whines Frank sitting beside Lou, his eyes red and puffy, a thin smile across his lips. "She doesn't drop either. Sure she's not a narc?"

"Hell no," says Chuck, aggravated. "She doesn't need drugs. She's on a spiritual high." He looks over at me, protective, putting his arm around me. I nod in agreement – knowing that it's more than that; remembering the night I tried a quarter tab of acid, found myself stunned by the beauty of the world, gasping at the illumination of headlights coming towards me on the road, wanting to merge completely with that light, the invisible divine; friends pulling me out of the street, worried; Chuck walking me home, protective and solemn; or the time I did inhale the reefer and found myself gasping for air, heart racing so fast I was sure I was dying, hardly able to walk, unable to talk, falling into bed crying and praying for salvation, begging Mother Mary to save me from the darkness descending.

"And we wouldn't be eating tonight if it weren't for her, our waifish pan-handlin' momma," chimes in Lou, grinning as he warms our dinner over the camp stove.

The stew tastes like heaven, like nothing so good has ever crossed my lips before. I eat until my stomach hurts, then lean back against the van to knit with the brown yarn and long wooden needles that Marty gave me before we left Missouri, frowning as she handed them to me. "You'll need something to do in that van, so you don't go crazy." Then laughing, "Tell me why you're going on this quest? You're braver than me. I couldn't do it," she says, hugging me briefly then turning to follow Dave, her new husband, the guy she met in high school and married spring semester of our freshman year so she could drop out of college; a world that had gotten far too out of control for her comfort. She doesn't wait for me to answer, to tell her that I really have nowhere else to go; can't go home, can't go back to school, no place to live, can't find a job, and that maybe California will be a place to start again, work in a restaurant with Chuck, maybe.

Chuck reads to me from *Be Here Now* while we eat. "We live in the moment because we can," he says, then hugging me: "It doesn't matter where we are Sue. We have our life together already, in *this* moment," he offers me the last spoonfuls of the coveted stew. I eat it gratefully.

After dinner, Walter, tall and lanky with long straight hair and thick eyeglasses, asks me to walk with him. It's become a thing we do sometimes in the evenings after dinner, if there is dinner. He's older than the rest of us, a poet and a grad student. As we stroll through the tents and campers, past the children shrieking with delight on the merry-go-round, he pulls out the small well-worn notebook from his shirt pocket and flips through several pages of scribbled hand-writing to read me his entry from today.

Blinded by spires of light, I've looked away
as the unblemished blue splintered in all directions.
And I've backed away from the sheer
precipice, the infinite suddenly a fearful measure.
[From Remedies for Vertigo by Walter Bargen]

My head spins from his fine words, tantalizing and delicious, impossible as a sumptuous dessert; I want to eat those words, digest them, make them mine so they can weave back up through my veins and feed the world with beauty someday – like he does, like he will.

"Sue if you want to leave here, travel, I'll hitchhike with you," his voice is soft and sweet.

My heart stirs at his offer. But fear overwhelms me; fear of hitchhiking into the unknown, fear of not being smart enough for Walter - this gracious poet intimidating me with the beauty of his hand-scribbled words; and something in me so loyal to our California quest, to Chuck; utterly convinced that *Being Here Now* is what my soul needs.

Years later I learn that Walter, an award winning poet, is appointed to be first poet laureate of Missouri. My heart stirs to hear it, remembering our evening walks, his whispered readings, his invitation to escape, seductive and unbearable; lighting up the grim darkness of early evening, tempting me with infinite possibility.

That night, in the dim light of our camping lantern, Lou sets up the army surplus tent for himself, Frank and Walter. Chuck and I always sleep in the van, throwing our thin cotton sleeping bags down as cushions, the metal floor still hard and painful on my hips; I spend most nights looking out the windows to watch the moon move slowly across the open sky, sending silent prayers to the vast unknown.

Just as the sun comes up, Lou's boisterous voice breaks the stillness, "I've got hot coffee! Let me in!" he bangs on the door and Chuck rises to open it. "That lady with the RV gave me a jar of Nescafe," he says happily, "I heated water on the camp stove, have some," passing the steel canteen cups to Chuck and me. "We'll get to San Francisco today," he shouts, exuberant, cranking up the Pink Floyd. "I've got windowpane for the Golden Gate Bridge!"

I close my eyes and remember crossing the Golden Gate Bridge one year ago, exactly, but a different lifetime. Vivid memories flood my senses, bringing tears to my eyes that I quickly wipe away.

June 1969 – Los Angeles and San Francisco

In this long ago lifetime, this distant memory from a year ago, Crissie and I are in the back seat of her parents rental car, driving across the long red sweep of the Golden Gate bridge, gasping at the startling beauty around us; a blend of emerald green sloping hillsides and sapphire blue water whipped into frothy foam; the sudden thick grey fog wrapping around our car, Crissie's dad laughing and pointing out the dim sunlight shining through the break of clouds above us, his hands gripping the steering wheel, driving us carefully across the bridge, his face grinning with delight.

We'd stayed at the Ritz Carlton then, eating at the finest San Francisco restaurants; "I love the way you're such an adventurous eater Sue," he'd said cheerfully patting me on the back when I agreed to try something new; the lamb or the sourdough; Crissie turning her nose up at whatever he put on her plate to taste, rolling her eyes at me.

Later Crissie's mom takes me to high tea in the hotel lobby. Crissie and I had been tired, cranky, arguing over something silly in the back seat as we pulled up to the hotel. "Have tea with me, Sue," said her mother navigating us into the hotel's restaurant as Crissie rode the elevator to our room.

"Everything feels better after a good cup of hot tea, don't you agree?" she asks smiling, her melodious southern voice soothing as she pours steaming English Breakfast into my porcelain china tea cup. "Tell me about the classes you'll be taking in the fall, Sue, when you start at the University. MU is a great school, perfect for your writing."

I recite the array of required courses from English 101 to American History and French. "Good, good," she says kindly, "I think you'll be happy there, become a writer. Give it time though, it'll be a big campus, probably different from anything you've known before. Just give it time," she adds more hot tea to my cup, then pauses, thoughtful, adds a sugar cube to her cup. "Crissie will be overwhelmed a bit at first too," she says softly. "Especially at Georgetown, it's a challenging school, especially for this first class of women," she shakes her head. "Oh you girls, you'll do fine, you'll have wonderful lives." She puts her cup down on the saucer, looks directly at me, and reaches across the table to take my hand, "Please call me, or call Crissie, any time you need to talk to someone," her voice warm and sweet like the tea, filling me with hope.

Crissie's mom had been my high school counselor, patiently guiding me through the process of applying to colleges that might consider a shy insecure girl from Convent of Mercy high school in Mobile, Alabama - whose only strong point was writing. She'd encouraged University of Missouri because of Journalism, she said, something she thought I'd be good at, in a college that might accept me. And even though my writing was mostly poetry and fiction, I agreed. Bennington, my dream school, had rejected me, and University of Missouri was far enough away from the south to be exciting. With her help I was accepted.

She'd planned this summer trip to California to get us both comfortable with seeing new places, as she'd explained to my mother, "To get them used to being away from home." My mom and dad had worried that Crissie's parents were too liberal and that we'd see things in California that might encourage us in the wrong direction once we went off to college.

My parents were deeply disturbed by what they saw on ABC news in the evenings, the outrageous hippie summer of love in San Francisco, the emerging drug culture of the Haight-Ashbury district, young people rallying against the Vietnam war on college campuses, black rights activists stirring up trouble even in their conservative hometown of Mobile, Alabama.

They'd finally acquiesced because Crissie's mom was, after all, my English teacher and a guidance counselor at our Catholic high school; and hadn't we known them since I was 7 when Crissie and I became best friends; "Of course, of course, it'll be fine," promised Crissie's mom.

The trip had been exhilarating; flying into Los Angeles (my first airline flight) renting a car to drive the winding spectacular coastal roads, steep cliffs falling away from the narrow highway down to a tumultuous blue sea so different from the tame and murky Gulf of Mexico I was used to; Crissie and I smiling and waving at the long haired scruffy kids who peered into our car as we drove the sunset strip; Crissie's mom delighted by the little shops whose store fronts displayed fashions we'd never seen before; suede fringed vests, large floppy leather hats, vividly colored dresses so short they barely covered the mannequin's "privates;" taking us shopping to buy the "adorable hippie hats and jackets" that I wore every day for the rest of our trip, running my fingers along the soft suede, thrilled with the promise of a future so far removed from my sterile childhood.

From the back seat of the car, Crissie and I marvel at the hundreds of hitch hikers, kids our age, long haired and rowdy, jutting their thumbs up towards heaven as our car slowly climbs the ramp to enter the California freeway; pushing away from the highway railing to wave their signs in front of our windshield, signs painted with the names of towns I've never been to: Las Vegas, Phoenix, Seattle.

Near the end of our trip, Crissie's dad finally agrees to buy us tickets to see Hair at the Aquarius Theater; "It's a once in a lifetime experience for them," urges Crissie's mom, grinning back at us. "She's right dad," says Crissie, looking over at me. "We'll never experience anything like this again," covering her face with her hand, laughing silently, a quick look over at me as we both fall into quiet giggles.

And now a year later, disowned by my parents for what exactly, I can't remember, marched against the war, grew my hair long, flunked my second semester while protesting on campus. Oh so many things, so many reasons to disown you, said my mother, you've shamed our family, and the way you dress, I just don't understand how you can make yourself so ugly; my dad driving up by himself to see where I lived in a messy, happy house with hippies in every room, all of us long haired and innocent, sharing everything we owned. He cries when he says good-bye. I can't go home with you dad, I can't, because of mom, I cry in his arms. I know, he says sadly, I know.

This trip was to be our grand adventure - to live in California, get jobs, share a house, be here now. Driving across the Golden Gate Bridge with *Let it Be* echoing from the speakers, I close my eyes and sing along, *There will be an answer, Let it Be, Let it Be.*

From the driver's seat Lou is animated, jumpy, describing the rainbow colors he's seeing on the bridge: "It's from the windowpane, wow, it's wild, do you see it?" his laughter fading when I ask him to pull over as soon as we cross the bridge because

Chuck is having a panic attack, curled beside me on the floor of the van, his eyes dilated from the windowpane they all took an hour ago.

We pull to the side of the road after the bridge and they all stumble out except for Chuck and me; I prop him up against the back of a seat and hold a chocolate chip cookie in front of his face, "Look at this Chuck, it's your favorite, take a bite." After some persuasion, his eyes finally focus and he bites into the cookie, chewing as tears roll down his cheeks, "Thank you, thank you," he says, "I can feel my body now." But his eyes are still wild and dilated and it's not until the sun rises and the others stumble back into the van that I'm convinced Chuck will be okay. It's the last time he ever drops acid.

As the sun rises over the bay, I finally know that it's not this; that my life lies somewhere between this chaos and the soul sucking orderliness of my mom's house. Holding the white rosary beads in my fingers I pray silently to Mother Mary to bring me home, wherever that is. I'm taking a stand for the light I realize, exhausted from helping Chuck fight his demons all night; finished with the darkness. Finally.

Cat Stevens' soothing voice from the speakers…

From the moment I could talk I was ordered to listen.

Now there's a way and I know that I have to go away.

I know I have to go…

We're offered a place to crash at someone's farm near San Rafael, on a hillside overlooking the city where they grow "organic" vegetables (what is that? I ask Chuck who doesn't know either). In a house filled with white things, people wearing white clothes, we weed in the gardens to fund our trip back to Missouri. An older guy, bearded and longhaired, who lives in the house, works beside me in the garden, teaching me which plants to keep and which to pull. After awhile he says kindly; "You're just a couple years too late, you know. You missed the good stuff in the city. It's all chaos now. That's why we moved to the country, to build something real."

A pony-tailed, peaceful-looking woman with a kind face is doing yoga in the living room one morning and asks me to join her; it feels like a light piercing through my heart, a salvation in the midst of condemnation; Yes it's this, it's this, I cry silently - following her through a series of uncomfortable yet somehow familiar postures in the spacious living room, sunlight rising up through the corn stalks and tomato plants in the garden to shine in through the bay window, illuminating our hands, palms together, fingers pointing towards the sky in Prayer Pose, tears of happiness streaming down my cheeks.

Now there's a way and I know that I have to go away...

June 1971 – Columbia, Missouri

One year later I'm living on an organic farm commune in Missouri. We rent the house and the land and call it Stoneybrook. We planted two acres of vegetables in the spring, hardly knowing what we were doing, fueled with optimistic ideas and boundless enthusiasm. Kneeling amidst the vivid green rows of leafy lettuce as the sun rises hot and sweet against my face; weeding around the spindly carrot tops, a scent of freshly blooming marigolds, spicy and tart, flooding my senses; surveying the rows and rows of promise, I'm filled with hope, happy with life.

I work days in town at a café, once a burger joint, where we now serve homemade grain burgers, freshly baked carrot cake, guacamole sandwiches on whole wheat bread baked late into the night and salads made from lettuce just picked that morning. We have lines of customers around the block, college students hungry for something new and different. I spend my extra time visiting the only "health food" store in town; sitting amongst the dusty bookshelves, reading about vitamins to cure colds, herbs for bladder infections, natural remedies to bring down fevers, the merits of apple cider vinegar. Richard, the aging store owner, knows me; lets me sit there reading for hours, gladly answers all my questions about this new way of eating and these natural remedies that can heal anything that ails you.

We have weekly meetings in the front yard of Stoneybrook, cross-legged in a circle, Dave strumming his guitar, Dan passing the reefer. "I agree that this is the right land to buy," says Ron.

"But we need to get the price down so we can pay it off quickly." Luke nods in agreement, passing around the documents that would seal the deal, purchase 300 acres of farmland near the Missouri river, just south of here, turn it into a trust that no one could ever own or sell. The land will cost $30,000.

We gather every Sunday on this newly purchased land to share potlucks made mostly from beans, rice, salads and home made breads; lining up to sign the ledger that records how much we've each been able to save during the week and donate towards "liberating the land." Chuck is long gone, living and working in California; my new love, Jeff, hair longer than mine, shows me a secluded plot on the new land where he wants to build us a railroad-tie home, something he read about in a catalog and now spends hours sketching in a notebook. We all dream of creating a sustainable life on this land, growing our food, building solar powered homes, living in community, simple and free, removed from a world that seems empty and without purpose.

Within 3 years we've paid the $30,000 loan off completely and we own the land in a trust, free and clear. But the price of buying the land has sent most of us into town, looking for better jobs, more money, which turns out to be a good thing for me – becoming a Montessori pre-school teacher, Jeff working two jobs to help pay for my training. Now I spend my days standing amidst a classroom of toddlers, helping them sound out vowels, count spindles into a box, paint an abstract giraffe, put order into a chaotic world; it heals me.

I hold one of my students, 3-year old Molly, in my lap as she sounds out each letter on the page; "C... A... T..." moving my index finger across the three letters again, quicker this time, and she slurs the sounds together, then suddenly looks up at me, a startled recognition of the word cat. "CAT," she says, excited, a jumble of new words now pouring from her lips as she turns each page of the book, putting vowels and consonants together to form each word.

"I'm reading, Sue" she says quietly, "I'm reading," afraid to look at me and break the magic spell until the book is finished; closing it carefully, then wrapping her small arms around my waist, both of us joyful; "You can read Molly! You can read!"

Knowing I've done something good, trying to do something helpful every day; this particular moment golden, rising up out of me to mingle in the light somewhere above in the vast unknown, my vapor of happiness rising.

August 1969 - Long Beach, Mississippi - just before the hurricane

My dad is sitting on an old wicker chair on the screened porch facing the sea, a bottle of Barq's root beer, foamy and wet, on the floor beside him, legs crossed gracefully, one foot kicking a soundless rhythm, long thin fingers deftly weaving nylon fishing line through a tiny hole he just made at the top of a hollow branch of sugar cane cut fresh from our lot next door; he reaches over occasionally to the ashtray on the floor beside him to take a drag on his Viceroy, "It's a new fishing pole for Roy," he says, thin blue smoke curling from his mouth as he exhales, "we'll use it later when the weather clears. I'll make you one too."

"Okay daddy," I answer without looking up from my book. I'm down the porch from him, on the old wooden swing, the one Grandpa built years ago, hung from the ceiling so we could all sit together on the humid evenings, catching a soft breeze from the water, mosquitos buzzing against the screens while we jumbled on top of each other, arms and elbows everywhere, singing along to his favorite tunes; *Take me out to the ballgame, take me out with the crowd, buy me some peanuts and cracker jacks, I don't care if I never get back.*

I'm reading Franny and Zooey again, loving the sound of the drizzle, steady and percussive on the wooden roof, loving the way it contains us in the house, pulls us in from the beach to watch the squalls move across the distant water in front of the house, the low lazy sweep of shallow that we were all just playing in, running from sandbar to sandbar to chase the minnows; almost beat Russell to the deep water markers just hours ago, waves once gentle now whipped into foamy rolling white caps.

Dad keeps glancing up at those waves and the distant sparks of lightening on the horizon, a contented smile on his face, inhaling deeply from his Viceroy, shaking his head at the sound of my two brothers fighting over a game of Parcheesi in the house, the smell of my Grandma's fresh crab gumbo, rich and peppery, rolling towards us from the kitchen far back inside the house.

My dad loves these squalls, always brings me to the porch to sit with him on stormy afternoons; Sue, you can smell the pine trees on Cat Island; inhaling deeply, closing his eyes to listen to the rush of whitecaps rolling towards the beach, pointing out the fierce billowy grey clouds skimming across the horizon. We both sit quiet, occupied, happy. From next door, a loud bang like someone slamming against a wall, then Aunt Bee Dee's shrill voice rising, urgent, scolding my cousins Russell and Davis, telling them to settle down, stop fighting, read their comic books or they'll get a spanking.

The screen door swings open and Grandpa joins us on the porch, stopping to adjust the squeaky spring, fiddle with the hinge, mumbling about how he just oiled it yesterday, turning to look long and hard at the distant water, quiet, thoughtful, "Tommy we need to bring the boats in today, before you all leave tomorrow." My dad nods, "Okay dad," he says, his voice is low and gravelly with smoke.

Then facing me, pausing for a moment, Grandpa's Irish blue eyes bright, amused, his weathered face cracks into a big grin:

"Hot damn, Sue Ellen, always with a book. You'll be a writer someday, won't you," he comes to sit beside me on the swing, his white cotton pants deeply wrinkled, his white shirt showing signs of dark grease from the boat engine he was just working on in his tool shed behind the house; not a tool shed really, more like a church, his altar - where dozens of meticulously cleaned and polished tools hang in their precisely outlined places along the weathered walls; instead of incense, the air is filled with the pungent scent of motor oil, thick and spicy as the Chinaberry tree outside the entrance.

On sweaty summer afternoons, I love visiting him in his cool orderly sanctuary, tiptoeing carefully across the rusted sheet of iron salvaged from his ferry boat that flanks the drainage ditch around the shed; always hoping to surprise him, enter soundlessly to watch him work, but never quite able to prevent the noisy clang of bending metal at the door, the gong that alerts him of visitors; his surprised smile welcoming and unconditional, his hands still on the wheel of the sander or holding a well-oiled bolt just selected from his collection inside a used cigar box, its lingering tobacco aroma rising to mingle with the persistent scent of turpentine.

Today, sitting beside me on the swing, he smells of engine grease, Chinaberries, and Dr. Tichenor's minty cure-all that he rubs into his swollen hands every morning.

"You're not really going away to college, are you?" he asks, teasing. "Yes sir," I answer awkwardly, never sure what to say, smiling at him. "In two weeks," I add, hoping to keep him talking and sitting on the swing beside me. He pats my knee, clumsy and brief, but somehow sentimental; his way of showing affection, unable to say the words, but the wide smile, the moist eyes, giving him away. He is after all, the tough Irish ferry-boat captain Ralph Peter O'Malley the "man of the river," as he's known in New Orleans.

"She's going to Missouri," says my dad from across the porch, looking up from his fishing line, briefly smiling at me as he takes a swig of foamy root beer.

"Why so far?" says Grandpa shaking his head back and forth; It's not a question to be answered, just a comment, and feeling shy and awkward as always I say nothing; just smile, happy to sit beside him as he pushes the swing back and forth with his feet.

He looks over at the water again, studying the thick clouds to the east and west. "I think it's going to be a big storm," he says. "We're due. But we're fine here, no hurricane has ever hurt us, these homes are built strong." I nod and say, "Yes sir," having heard these stories so many times, the way his father John Peter O'Malley bought this land at the turn of the century, built these two sturdy homes for the O'Malley clan, side by side, separated by an oyster shell driveway with ancient water oaks reaching protectively over each house, gracing the long driveway with silvery moss.

From as far back as I can remember, dad filled my head with Long Beach. Instead of nursery rhymes to send me to sleep, his bedtime tales were of childhood summers and long weekends "across the lake" playing all day in the warm Mississippi water with his two older brothers; hauling Grandpa's hand-made nets to the rock pile to catch jumbles of blue claws for Grandma's spicy gumbo, chasing minnows in the shallow pools, finding cold freshwater springs bubbling up impossibly through the sandbars, good enough to drink. And when the afternoon high tide rolled back in, launching their sailboats and dinghies to race each other, capsizing in the summer squalls, sometimes making it all the way to Cat Island.

I hungered for these stories; tell me more, I pleaded, about when there wasn't a beach and the water came right up to the sea wall; or how your mom got mad because Grandpa named the skiff Salty Dog instead of Ruth, or how you and your brothers would beg and plead in the back seat on the way home to New Orleans until Grandpa stopped for chocolate malts at Little Man's.

Dad would acquiesce, lighting up another cigarette, leaning back against the headboard, happy to have an audience; describing how he couldn't pay attention in class because all he thought about was getting back to the warm shallow Gulf, the earthy smell of mossy oaks, the wooden dinghy he was helping his brothers build; all of it dreamy and true, yet somehow too good, too impossible; a place to long for.

He found his soul in Long Beach, he told me, felt God's presence in the moonlight streaming through the windows, luminous stars reflected on the foamy waves, sugar cane swaying and cracking in the lot next door; Long Beach was holy ground for my father who once dreamed of becoming a priest.

It had become my altar too, confessing my darkest adolescent desires, guilty Catholic sins, to the brilliant stars above the pale sand; climbing high into the water oak at the top of the yard; its trunk so wide we could play tag around it, branches twisted and majestic; it held Russell and I safe no matter how high we climbed, no matter how big we grew; straddled beside each other on its rough and knotted limbs to survey the miles of silver beach, pointing out white sails dotting the flat horizon, mesmerized by the endless flow of shallow waves along the shore, the distant outline of tall trees on Cat Island; calculating how far away the afternoon squalls were by counting seconds between the distant flash of lightning and the slow rumbling heavy thunder, holding our arms tightly around the Oak branch where we sat as the wind kicked up; daring each other to stay even when electric flashes lit the air around us. This land was my goddess, my Holy Communion, my respite from Mobile.

Mom rarely made it to Long Beach; too crowded with everyone piled into two small bedrooms in back, she explained, and the kitchen so hot and muggy, the house so old and dirty; not a place she could ever get clean. She made brief visits, uncomfortable and nervous, fussy and angry, until dad would drive her and my younger sister Ann back to Mobile.

Later I understood that mom never had a chance at Long Beach; she wasn't born with the ease of a yachtsman; the ability to find equilibrium on water was lost to her; instead of striking a handsome pose on the bow of a boat as it cruised into harbor like Aunt BeeDee; mom spent her time hanging from the stern puking her guts out until her feet were firmly back on land.

And much later I recognized the coolness of these logical left-brain sailors, these O'Malley men with their watery eyes and Kennedy-ish voices, their aloof charisma; it obliged women like my mom no entry into a conversation. If a thing wasn't logical it was of little value. Hours were spent over dinner reviewing the best way to mend a hull; tune an engine; hoist a sail; weather patterns were announced and debated over coffee every morning.

My mom knew none of those words even though she tried hard at first to engage with their cleverness but as her duties bound her to motherhood her youngest girl Ann became her refuge, a safe place to be. And still it was more than that; her French Creole otherness was alien to Uncle Warren, Aunt BeeDee and their brood. Although I could not see this at the time; my mom never had a chance at Long Beach.

For me, the half-breed, it was different; I'd been raised to love water; was cherished as part of the worthy O'Malley clan because I carried the correct last name; and finding my equilibrium on a rocking boat was something I mastered early when dad taught me to focus on the horizon – always the horizon. He raised me to love Long Beach.

And there were ghosts of course, the spirits of departed O'Malleys walking the creaky floors at night; all of us kids gathered around Grandpa as he told stories of seeing his dead father, John Peter, walking through the bedrooms, making us laugh and scream with delight, afraid to go to bed; but I'd seen him too, the bodiless white cotton shirt floating across our rooms in the dark; sweet and benevolent, making sure we were safe.

But the spirits I felt in the house most often were the never-mentioned daughters; my dad's only two sisters, Muriel and Ruthie, born long before he was, both of them suddenly ill in their adolescence, doctors not knowing why, putting them in wheelchairs to spend their last summers in Long Beach hoping for a cure, until they both died before the age of 18; my father, the youngest, having no memory of them, their names rarely mentioned in the family.

I felt their presence most when dad sent me back to the house alone at night to get salt for our watermelon or buns for the hotdogs, all of us sitting jumbled and happy along the concrete sea wall that led down to the beach, sharing thick curved slices of watermelon, chewing down to the rind, chins dripping with sweet red nectar, spitting the dark seeds at each other; my Grandpa hauling dead branches out from the woods behind our house to build the tallest bonfires we'd ever seen, taller than my dad, so we could wave sparklers, shoot fire crackers, punch each other late into the night under the stars on the warm sand, barefoot since sunrise; tiptoeing back towards the house obedient, alone, afraid; seeing Muriel and Ruthie's faces in the tiny attic window above the porch; singing as loud as I could to alert them, tell them I was there; a kind of permission I needed to enter their dark sanctuary, knowing in my bones how they loved this house, this land; their spirits never leaving for heaven, no reason to go, this was, after all, better than anywhere.

Grandpa stands up now, walks the length of the porch, studying the sky above the water, "We'll have a break in the storm this afternoon, Tommy, let's get ready to go," he says, something in his voice anxious, worried, a twisting I feel in my gut, a sudden dropping of the stomach for no reason, a thing unknown, or known but not spoken. Grandpa slowly turns to go back into the house, smiling over at me one last time, those brilliant sapphire eyes framed in delicate round glasses, his stark white hair strangely luminescent in the rainy light; this image becoming one of my strongest memories from that day.

"Run and get Warren and the boys," says my dad gently, putting his cigarette out in the metal ashtray, laying the cane pole carefully along the edge of the porch. "Yesssir," I answer eagerly, closing my book, relieved to have a task, to feel included.

For the rest of the stormy wind-whipped day, my dad, his brother Warren, my brothers Roy and Micky, my cousins Russell and Davis and myself all wrestle with the odd collection of wooden boats anchored in the salty shallows needing to be hauled back to the house for winter; including the ancient skiff named Salty Dog and Uncle Warren's slick new racing yacht, The Indigo, that he and Russell sailed over from New Orleans earlier in the summer.

Uncle Warren sends Russell and me out to where the Salty Dog is anchored, the old wooden skiff rocking crazily in the waves. We gladly obey, trudging side by side against the whitecaps until the water reaches our chests and I'm jumping up on tiptoe to keep my head above each wave. Russell glances over, "Stay here Sue Ellen," he orders as he makes the final steps to the boat. But I don't listen, wanting to be there when he reaches up for the side of the skiff and heaves himself over, losing balance briefly in the waves, then grinning down at me and reaching over to pull me up with one arm; both of us grinning, chuckling, nervous, excited by the wind, the silvery color of the air.

We're the same age, born months apart in side-by-side duplexes Grandpa bought on Canal Boulevard in the heart of New Orleans, right on the streetcar line; friends since our mothers bundled us together in carriages to stroll through Audubon Park, or take the little train around the zoo. Russell carries the Irish blood of our Grandpa, fair skin freckled by the sun, straight dark hair cut short against his head, sky-blue eyes reflecting light even on rainy afternoons; I'm dark eyed and olive skinned, deeply tanned from the first day of summer.

"Get the oars ready, Matey!" he barks, from the front of the boat – assuming the voice of a crusty sea captain, dreaming of a future in the Navy like his dad.

He leans over the bow, the choppy water rocking us side to side as he pulls up the thick frayed rope that leads to the anchor, the boat facing into oncoming waves, salt spray peppering our faces; he heaves the rusted anchor aboard and yells at me from over his shoulder to start rowing. I try to get the bulky wooden oars coordinated against the waves but to no avail and the sea knocks us sideways, pushing us closer to shore, nearly capsizing us in the swells until he secures the anchor, grabs the oars from my hands, and without much effort, turns our boat to face the rock pile, rowing us steadily across the turbulent surf; both of us wind whipped, soaking wet and grinning, loving the cold drizzle on our cheeks, the thrill of lightning in the distance, the air charged with fear and anticipation until we arrive at the rock pile and Uncle Warren tosses us a rope.

It's a windy day, squalls moving in and out, Grandpa's white hair pushed straight up whenever he faces the horizon, delicate eyeglasses dotted with sea water, an anxious expression on his face, yelling orders at Warren, who then yells them at us; bring me that rope, secure that line, help me carry this anchor; all of us struggling to get our tasks done in the chaos, to hear his voice above the thunder, the sound of Davis yelling that he *is* tying the knot correctly, Russell shouting over at Davis, Uncle Warren calling someone stupid, my dad yelling at everyone to stop fighting; the men now a chorus of angry shouting that rises sharp and disturbing through the pounding rain. I feel stupid, inept, unable to handle the heavy oars, help carry the anchor, be important enough to get yelled at.

The next day when dad finishes packing our station wagon with suitcases and fishing gear, Micky, Roy and I stand nervously by the car, not wanting to pile in, picking up oyster shells from the driveway to bring home in our pockets for the long drive along Highway 90 to Mobile.

Grandpa and Grandma give us quick hugs, my Grandma moist with perspiration in her long cotton dress, low heels, smelling of brushed powder, rich and fruity. Grandpa tells my dad not to worry, that they'll only stay in Long Beach one more day before heading back to New Orleans for their flight to California to visit their oldest son Pete who moved there a decade ago to become a naval architect.

Standing beside our car, Uncle Warren and Russell argue about whether to drive back to New Orleans tomorrow with Aunt BeeDee and Davis or to sail their boat home; not sure if it might be safer to sail into Gulfport for the pending storm; stopping their argument long enough to look into our car windows, Russell smiling over at me, "Bye cuz, be good at college." "You too," I answer, "Send me a postcard if you have time," I yell out the window as our car backs down the driveway.

Davis stands on the highway median to wave good-bye like always, lighting a firecracker and tossing it high into the air for our farewell; Russell, Uncle Warren, and Aunt BeeDee walk alongside our car, closing the gate behind us as we pull out onto the road.

From the back seat, windows down, we wave and yell good-bye, throwing kisses as the car pulls away, already beginning to cry as we pass the old St. Thomas church on the corner, sick with regret that summer is ending, that we're heading home to Mobile where mom awaits with our younger sister Ann and school is about to start.

In the gloomy quiet of the back seat, I dream of our annual Easter weekend returns to Long Beach; how we run outside early in the morning right after mass at St. Thomas Church to find our hand-dyed Easter eggs hiding in Grandpa's rose bushes or in the cavernous roots of the Oak tree; the younger kids screaming and pushing each other out of the way to grab the jelly beans and gold nugget candy bars before we change into bathing suits to spend the day racing on the warm sand, chasing minnows between the sand bars, building our first sand castle of the year.

But none of this is ever true again.

What Grandpa senses happens in the next few days, after he and Grandma have flown to California to visit Uncle Pete; and even though none of us are lost in the hurricane, it changes him, eats away at his insides when he returns to see our land scraped clean of any trace of us, dish towels hanging from the tops of oak trees.

Everyone is found safe after the storm, even though Uncle Warren and Russell stayed another night to secure their boat, tried to sleep as the water began to rise, electrical explosions from the neighbor's house waking them to stand on the porch and see the Gulf of Mexico rolling into our yard. They'd somehow made it inland to higher ground at the Anderson's bicycle shop until the waves retreated in the morning and they stumbled back to find the land unrecognizable, too stunned to speak, hanging onto each other, sobbing like children.

That day of leaving for summer's end in 1969 is the last day we ever stand around the oyster shell driveway, hugging and fighting, watching Davis light the farewell firecracker, waving at Grandpa at the gate, eyes moist, arms crossed, shaking his head.

As we drive the long wordless trip to Mobile, Hurricane Camille is already gathering strength in the Atlantic, making its predicted turn into the Gulf of Mexico, stalled by the warm water; furious clouds spinning waves into a frenzy from three feet to 30 feet high by the time they roll through our yard, slice limbs from the Oak trees, scatter the oyster shell driveway, lift Grandpa's sturdy homes from their concrete foundations and smash them angrily on the railroad tracks two blocks inland; Grandpa's tool shed vanished completely, leaving only the metal sheet that once noisily marked its entrance.

Back home in Algiers, Grandpa is never quite the same; rising in the mornings to fumble with his white cotton shirt, telling Grandma to wake up "it's time to drive across the lake;" his memory, his mind as smashed and scattered as his once sacred tools. He dies a few years later from a stroke.

More than a week after the storm, when the roads have been cleared of enough debris that dad can finally drive us over, we find one rusted wrench from Grandpa's tool shed laying on the ground where the Chinaberry tree once stood; my dad climbs silently through piles of splintered branches, steps carefully over a shattered kitchen table leg and across an oddly bent piece of wood from the porch swing to find it; saying nothing, shaking his head and turning to walk away from us.

It marks the end of most good things for a very long time. Russell leaves for college a week after the storm, joins ROTC, trains to be a navy pilot, is sent to Vietnam. His younger brother Davis, troubled and searching, takes off for parts unknown to become a musician, is mostly disowned by his parents.

My dad drives over to Long Beach by himself on weekdays, secret detours from his business trips, taking Polaroids of the disheveled land; filling our family albums with pages of devastation.

I leave for my freshman year at University of Missouri the next week; haunted by images of Long Beach floating away; startled awake each night as the 30 foot wall of water tumbles towards me; grieving for what I've just lost – not fully understanding yet that it was everything.

Long Beach is never rebuilt; property values plummet after the storm; insurance companies refuse to pay for water damage. Our lots stand empty and forlorn well into the early 90s when they're divided up and sold to condo developers.

Later Hurricane Katrina sweeps in and restores grace; clears away the soulless condos and leaves our land vacant and sacred, the battered and hollowed remnants of our two majestic water oaks standing guard.

10

THE GIFT

Rollinsville, Colorado – Summer 1992

"Give me something hard to do," I say to Babaji, sitting cross-legged at his feet in the sunroom after breakfast. It's Saturday July 13 – twelve years to the day since Paul slipped away, flew out the window, got scattered into a mountain lake, lifted me to the other side.

"Ah," Babaji sighs, "So many things come to mind." He laughs, then closes his eyes, inhales, circulates his breath, fingers moving across his coral mala beads, "We're building a Ma Shrine. It's a temple to the divine feminine." He opens his eyes, smiles broadly, "We're getting a large Lakshmi Murti from India, Brian's coordinating the crew to build a temple for it." Then looking down at me, "We need to clear a trail leading to it, line it with nice boulders."

"Sounds like my kinda work Babaji," I laugh, nodding to him, grateful for the task.

The day is warm, high altitude sun blazing in my eyes as I step outside; the thin ravenous air sucking my breath away as I walk uphill, following the deep echo of hammers pounding on 2 x 4s.

Brian and his crew are working on the temple's frame; he waves when he sees me. There are eight young guys working along side of him, all of them Babaji's students. When I explain the task Babaji outlined, he smiles sweetly. "Why don't you pick someone from this group to help you Sue. Those boulders are heavy."

I agree. A young guy with shaggy blonde hair steps forward; he's new to the Sangha, offers to help and follows me to the shed to gather tools we'll need; work-gloves, wheelbarrow, hoe, shovel, pitch fork. "The ground is rock hard," I explain. "We have to really dig down to uproot the plants."

He's quiet, shy, as we collect everything and head to the new building site. We mark off a gently curving trail leading from the main road slightly uphill to where the new temple is being built.

I ask his name. "I'm John O'Malley," he smiles and extends his hand. "Glad to meet you. I just arrived up here a couple weeks ago." His vowels are jangly and drawled, stretched out like a lazy afternoon in a small southern town when there's absolutely nothing to do.

"Are you from Alabama?"

"Heck yeah," he grins.

"And your name is John O'Malley; like my great grandpa John Peter O'Malley; and your eyes are stupid blue and your hair is blonde and messy like Christopher's; and give me a break you're from the south; and here you are in the middle of nowhere in Colorado, on this day of July 13, which is my day; always my day. This must be Paul's little joke for me," I laugh.

"What?" he asks, wide-eyed and hesitating.

"Never mind. Just follow me and do what I say. You'll be fine. How'd you get here?"

"Hitch-hiked. Met some folks in Boulder and told them I wanted to meditate; they sent me here."

"Of course," I shake my head and laugh. "We have lots of work to do. Let's get going."

I teach him to use the hoe to break up the dirt clods, pull up the yarrow and sage, set them aside to replant later; then smooth out the dirt, flatten it into a walk-able surface. He's not used to physical labor and soon sits down in the shade of a tree to rest.

"Why do you care so much?" he asks.

"About this trail?" I look over at him under the tree; he looks discouraged, lost.

"This work, all of it, everything." He looks away, towards the ridge.

"It's a blessing to be here, in this air, John," I say moving to sit beside him. "It's removed from the world. Soak it up. Let it heal you. When you leave here, the pieces that are true will stay with you. For now just surrender to it."

"Why do they value this hard physical labor so much?" he asks, his voice sincere.

"We do it to surrender ego, to lose ourselves. Hard physical work is joyful when you feel you're doing it for a higher purpose, for Nityananda. I'm building this trail for Nityananda and Lakshmi. So I want it to be sweet for them, because they've made my life so sweet. Does that make sense?"

He smiles at me, "Not really. But I'll give it a try."

I ask him about his family in Alabama and he tells me stories of an overbearing father; a successful southern attorney who wants John to become a lawyer and follow the family legacy. "That's not what I want my life to be," he says, shrugging his shoulders. "There has to be more than that."

"There is honey, there is. Trust me. You just have to go your own way to find it." I pull him up from the ground, bring him over to the trail to get back to work.

"The church I grew up in," he says, picking up the shovel, "it was all about fear and punishment. I don't believe in that kind of God. I'm trying to figure out what I do believe. I'm 21 and I don't want to live somebody else's life." He looks over at me, "And I've always been a little different," he grins. "Never sat well with my dad."

"Well, you've come to the right place," I laugh pulling hard on the roots of a large Artemisia plant that lives right in the center of our new trail, the spicy scent of sage rising around us, "Hmm, come smell this. It's one of my favorite herbs," I call out, handing him a leaf to inhale the tingly scent.

"Wow," he says again, surprised.

"Yeah, let's replant this in a good spot. Hemingway used to drink absinthe when he was a young writer living in Paris; it came from this plant and was apparently some sort of hallucinogenic back then. And addictive," I grin over at John. He nods, interested now.

"How do you know this stuff?" he asks. "I'd like to know more about plants." He tells me that he drops acid most weekends with his friends back home trying to have spiritual experiences.

"Well, I'm not sure that's the best way to connect to the divine," I laugh. "My generation thought it was and it didn't work out for us." He sits down on one of the boulders and says; "Tell me everything; tell me what you learned from that."

Only if we work while we talk, I answer, carrying our freshly uprooted Artemisia over to a prominent spot beside the new temple door. As we dig into the earth to plant it, I share stories from the past, explain what brought me to Shambhava.

"Wow," he whispers. "I want to have a life like yours; figure it out my way."

"It's the path less traveled, for sure. But it's not the easy way, not the easy path," I say looking at him directly, wanting him to understand the journey he's embarking on; remembering the older man years ago on my trip to California who taught me to find peace through weeding a garden, and the lovely woman inviting me to do yoga in her living room.

"John the only advice I have for you is to keep choosing light over darkness. Everything comes down to that."

He nods thoughtfully listening to every word. As we haul more boulders to line the path, heave them into the wheelbarrow, roll them into position, the sun bears down hard. We take water breaks, sitting in the shade to continue talking. The trail, encouraged by our efforts, slowly takes shape.

During lunch in the dining hall, I feel his energy shifting; like he wants something more from me, transferring his need for love or approval onto me whom he now feels in sync with even though I'm twice his age.

"I hope I find a woman just like you someday," he says looking deep into my eyes. "Someone beautiful and wise who I can really talk to – like we're talking." He gives me a hug that lasts just a bit too long, feels a bit too delicious.

For a moment, I bask in the rush of sexual tension between us, feeling flattered that he likes me, this young boy with my father's last name and Christopher's blue eyes; is this perfect or terrible; a gift or a samsara?

After lunch, Brian calls out to John, asks him to come back over and help them finish the framing. I'm relieved to spend the next hour working by myself, doing mantra, surrendering to Nityananda, nodding to acknowledge the brief presence of Paul who appears on the steps of the new temple grinning at me, tipping his baseball cap, then as I look closer, disappears. "Hello beautiful soul, thank you for everything," I whisper, glad for the visit.

Later Brian sends a different guy over from his crew to help me finish the trail. I enjoy working beside this soulful quiet young man with a long ponytail and deep brown eyes who now lives here at the ashram, plays guitar in Babaji's band on Friday nights, and who Faith told me was once addicted to heroin before he found his way to Shambhava looking for redemption.

After a couple more hours of digging up sage, cactus, and pine shrub and hauling more boulders into place, the path finally looks welcoming; gently bending from road to temple door. Brian and his guys have finished the framing and are working on the roof and walls. I'm amazed how quickly the small temple is taking form.

Near the end of the day as the sun begins to set behind the tall pines, I put my tools down, take my shoes off and walk inside; the air smells fresh and balmy, like newly-cut timber and crushed yarrow. It already seems to hold the spirit of the divine feminine; a warm glow rising from its bright pine floor.

I sit alone in the middle of the room, facing the spot reserved for the altar. Soon our six-armed, bejeweled and decorated Lakshmi will sit there, dazzling and seductive on her lotus blossom. Closing my eyes and I can see her, sense her arrival.

Brian sits beside me. "It's pretty nice in here, right?" he whispers. "You can feel the energy gathering."

"Feels like Lakshmi's blessing the space."

"Blessing us," he says, eyes closed, deeply inhaling. We sit silently for a few minutes, soaking up the stillness.

A breathy high-pitched breeze comes floating in through the unfinished windows; whining down from a faraway summit like a distant aria. I hear my mother's silvery voice calling my name: *Sue Ellen*. Startled, I open my eyes; search the small room, surprised that only Brian sits beside me.

The dinner bell gongs. Brian looks over, "I'm gonna put the tools away. See you at dinner." He takes off while I stay seated in meditation, my mother's voice lilting and melodious in the thin room as darkness flutters through. Evening birds call wistfully in the distance; mourning doves lovely and persistent, then a raven's cantata urgent and far away; my mother's face floating on the dappled light.

I've missed my mom, the whole crazy jumble of her; angry, abusive, mean and wounded, encouraging and kind; expressive dark eyes, a voice like spun sugar; a sound you craved, unforgettable and haunting. Does a girl ever stop wanting her mother's love?

We'd found a sort of peace as the years stretched away from Paul's early death and my time in Mexico; both of us reaching hard across the distance to find each other; grateful for a resting place in my rising success as a journalist in the late 80s. Long before I'd worked for New Times, I'd been a newspaper reporter and magazine writer for a cancer publication. My work on that magazine had filled her with pride.

And though I wrote about things that were foreign to her, cancer research, natural remedies, she was thrilled to hear about the day I spent in Malibu with film star and cancer survivor Jill Ireland at her beach house. When Jill later sent me a hand written thank you note saying she'd loved the cover story and especially loved our conversation "because it was real and honest" - my mother framed the note.

When I traveled to New York to interview a well-known cancer doctor, following him on rounds at First Presbyterian and later to his sprawling penthouse to meet his renowned medical researcher wife, mom wanted to know every detail of their apartment and how beautiful it was to gaze from their windows across the tree-tops of Central Park.

She'd clipped all my cover stories, keeping them in a special folder on a prominent shelf beside the family albums; sharing them with friends over lunch or on Fridays at the beauty parlor; her voice sweet and proud to talk about the adventures of her journalist daughter.

Sitting here now in the falling light of the empty Ma Shrine, the brief chill of evening urging me to sleep, I feel pulled out of myself, above the physical, seeing my unfinished life from a great distance; memories of mom weaving through the dusk.

Exhausted, stretching out on the hardwood floor to rest; the room becomes a half-dream, time pausing; my soul ascending into the infinite swirl.

It was confusing and yet true that mom was a monster and a goddess – flipping from one to the other with little warning. As a child I'd learned to read the signs, know when the shift was coming, when she'd change from gorgeous and kind to hateful and destructive; aware even then of a pattern; not joining us at the dinner table, eating chocolate bars and drinking Coca-Cola alone in the kitchen, too tired from cooking the meal, she'd say; angry silence rising up around her like lightning in the air before a summer squall.

She refused to see a doctor or therapist for her "nervousness" as dad called it, and once after a miscarriage, her gynecologist prescribed something "to help her get some rest." Things had gotten worse after that, her grim depression tainting my adolescence. There seemed to be no hope for any of us. Then she'd surprise me; take me shopping for a new dress for the high school dance, her voice uplifting, encouraging as we picked out clothes for my future.

No one had ever really tried to help her, seen inside her pain, understood her sense of failure and overwhelm; Catholic priests and Mobile psychologists were incapable of grasping the plight of trapped and desperate women of the 50s, suburban wives and mothers who seemed to have everything and yet had nothing.

She always seemed to find her way back to the light, surveying the damage she had done in her fall to darkness, picking up the pieces, restoring order to the household; yet stubbornly unable to fathom the inner pain her children carried into their world everyday. No one did really. All seemed well; our uniforms cleaned and freshly pressed; our home a thing of order and beauty; all of us playing volleyball, basketball, running track, my brother becoming a football hero; who would question the well-being of such a home.

Yet wasn't this the story of all women; all of us potently loving and profoundly angry at once? Perhaps it only mattered how well we walked the edge, how seldom we surrendered to the dark; what gifts we had gathered to keep us upright when things fell apart; how not to hide in the kitchen eating chocolate and drinking Coca Cola when the world was tilting; instead to reach up, arms stretched wide to the empty sky and have our hearts broken open in the light; to call in the grace and take a different posture completely - the prayer pose instead of the fetal position; or to become a healer instead of surrendering to the rage of human suffering.

Why was our shamanic knowingness rejected by this world, considered witchcraft, schizophrenia, hypersensitivity, emotionalism, depression when it was clearly the gift of seeing beyond the surface, pulling back the curtain to reveal the script, the playwright, the contracts we'd signed before the play began.

How deeply women understood that the unseen and unsaid is more real than real; and how seldom men seemed to grasp this – to see beyond appearance; most of them barely able to imagine our rage, consider our pain; instead calling it names, giving it labels, finding a drug to hush it.

I saw the same pattern in our moms' lives; Margaret's mother a wealthy beautiful lonely alcoholic married to a raging genius; Faith's mother widowed, overwhelmed and grief-stricken as a single mom, or my mother losing herself completely to fit in to my father's world; all of them on the same search for truth; unable to find the map that would lead them away from desperation.

Were we simply trying to master the dance of shadow and light; to see through the cracks in the world? Why were women unafraid of this dichotomy while men seemed terrified of the shadow? As Jung had pointed out - the shadow self is as necessary as the higher self; there's so much wisdom revealed in every dark night of the soul; great truths only uncovered when we disconnect from the world, allow our souls to linger in what we've lost.

And maybe this was why I was so drawn to the Hindu deities. Their Durgas, the scary gods who protected us from evil, were just as esteemed as the loving Lakshmi and the powerful Ganesha, remover of obstacles; and both sides of Shiva, destructive and life-giving, were equally celebrated. It seemed a more female friendly path than most; acknowledging our dance of shadow and light.

Why didn't I help her? Why didn't I recognize my mother's pain and love her through it? What if it had been me who had disliked her and not the other way around? Didn't I reject her ultimately?

I'd played victim this time. Yet it felt so old, so familiar with her; like the same drama had been enacted between us for centuries, exchanging roles through parallel time – neither of us finding the courage to love the other, to break the pattern.

And what part did my father play in our triangle? He was the one we both adored, fought over. But this time I'd had the blessing of a father's unconditional love while mom was burdened with the duties of householder. She'd said often enough that she'd never really wanted children, wanted to travel with dad, celebrate life in New Orleans. Yet it wasn't a possibility in the 50s was it? Both of them so entrenched in the expectations of their times.

If it had all been reversed, if I'd been the householder, wouldn't I have felt the same sting of jealousy when my husband loved my daughter so effortlessly and I struggled to survive a soulless suburban life?

I remembered the strange familiar that I felt with my mom in the 80s, long after Paul had died, when her kids were finally moved out and she had a respite of sorts, freedom from obligations. She'd redecorated her living room, turning it into a sacred space filled with Chinese heirlooms, artwork, porcelain vases, Foo Dogs; this woman who'd never left the south reaching back through time into something oddly familiar, not fully understanding how it was solace from her own past.

I'd teased her that she was remembering her lifetime as a Buddhist monk. She'd surprised me with the answer: "Probably so," she'd said as she arranged the red and gold Foo Dogs to face her front door, standing guard in the foyer; revealing so much about herself in the peaceful stillness of that strange and lovely room; remembering the way we'd both sit reading in the lamplight late into the night whenever I'd visit; a thing my father couldn't understand, how we loved the quiet light, the books in our hands, the excitement of stillness.

I had failed her, I realized. She had wanted a son to come first, looking like my dad with Irish eyes and dark sweeping hair; a perfect blue-eyed baby like my cousin Russell born just months before. This baby would be her calling card into the O'Malley clan. Instead I carried the colors of her French Creole father; the poor but sweet farmer who grew sugar cane, barely spoke English, and never brought his family out of poverty. She didn't want to be shamed or pitied anymore. She didn't understand that my dad loved her for her past, for her dark struggles, her unyielding determination to rise above the simple farming family she'd been raised in.

"You never want to dig deep into your family tree, Sue Ellen, you just don't know what you might find," she had warned, hushing me when I asked her to tell me more about her parents; learning years later from Aunt Ruby that their French speaking father had been a respected herbalist; knowing which plants to pick for any ailment; how to boil "flower tea" to fight the fever, or make a goldenseal poultice for the pox. Their family was always too poor to see a doctor; he had been their healer.

Why didn't I understand this? Help her feel loved when she felt so alone? Why couldn't I forgive her desperate need to rise above her past, to create order and sanctity in the home above all else? I was simply in the way, forgetting to take my shoes off at the door. It really wasn't personal; never about me.

And when our family moved to Mobile, she'd found herself isolated, condemned by the dismissive old money of upper-crust Mobile; their housewives stylishly dressed from head to toe; their obedient black maids, tired and heavy from raising white children. None of these Spring Hill wives ever worked; most of them married to surgeons or lawyers in the all-white parish of St. Ignatius, considered the best school in Mobile and the reason my parents had built our home on this hill.

It hadn't been that way in mom's New Orleans - where people of every color rode the streetcars, women had jobs, there were musicals and ballets to see every weekend; and humanity celebrated side by side in the French Quarter, eating po-boys and gumbo at Domilise's; red beans and rice at Arnaud's, oysters at Acme Oyster House, or shrimp creole at Broussards.

Yes she'd been cold and unyielding to me; a punishing unforgiving mother; never touching me except to painfully tug on my thick unmanageable hair; rolling it into torturous brush curlers to sleep on, burning it with home-made perms, all in the hopes I would acquire the 50s flip, the simple wave that would make me lovely enough for St Ignatius parish, allow me to slip unnoticed into their fair skinned hierarchy; my stubborn hair never quite learning its lesson, becoming the target of her endless frustration.

As a child, when we visited her New Orleans home I'd seen the way she was repulsed by the older men of her family, her brothers unemployed, broken, drinking whiskey around the kitchen table, loud and sorrowful; I sensed her fear, her wariness within this crowded household; the youngest child of twelve. Had these older drunken siblings once hurt her, shamed her, shut her heart down, leaving her untouchable for me?

Why couldn't I have seen this from early on? Why wasn't I wise enough to love her anyway? Isn't it possible to be forgiving from the very beginning?

I believe it is. I'd met children like that before; Molly from my Montessori classroom had been that way; wise and forgiving beyond her years, somehow accepting of her mother's struggles, her mother's neglect.

My sin, I saw clearly now, was in not reaching for wisdom in the midst of my painful childhood; not loving her enough; not choosing the good parts of my mother and forgiving the rest.

Help me Lakshmi to only see goodness, to ignore the dark. I want to live in the light, I call out in the silent room - my own words taking sound and form to startle me awake.

"Sue, Babaji wants to see you," Brian's voice at the door pulls me back into my body. "I've saved you some dinner," he says sitting beside me. "It's in the kitchen with your name on it. When you're ready, Babaji wants you to visit him on his private porch, behind their cabin."

"Wow," I say, feeling like I've just woken from too long a nap, realizing my face is wet from tears, gathering myself, finding my water bottle and shoes. "I've never been to their private house before."

Brian stands in the temple doorway pointing to the hill behind the lake, the cluster of tall pines encircling a small well-hidden cabin deep in the woods. "It's easy to find," he says.

Then looking down at the winding path that points our way out; "This new trail looks really nice."

"It was fun to work on," I say as we follow it to the road then downhill to the dining hall. Once inside, I visit the bathroom, run water on my face, grab a fleece jacket, skip the meal, and hurry to find my way to Babaji and Faith's home.

There's no path that I can see and the ground is rough, untamed, tricky in the early evening light; the moon just a plaintive glow behind a tree-darkened ridge.

My body aches from hauling rocks but it feels good to move; treading carefully through the uneven land, stepping over thorny shrubs, around small boulders. It grounds me; I slowly come fully awake. It's a good feeling after my disorienting meditation in the Ma Shrine.

I'm unsure why Babaji has called me to his private home; a tiny piece of me wonders if it has to do with the new Sangha member John O'Malley, or the anniversary of Paul, or the new shrine, or none of these things.

Following Brian's instructions, I walk around their house to the back where a private deck overlooks a rolling valley of rising trees. Climbing the deck stairs, I find Babaji unmoving as a Murti, sitting in silent meditation on his cushioned chair, the dim lamplight from inside spilling out through a window to illuminate his burnt sienna shawl.

I sit quietly at his feet, digging into my pockets to find the rosewood mala, settling into meditation, eyes closed. Time passes, doubles back again; I see my mother's face, young and beautiful, then Paul laughing, a brief glimpse of young John O'Malley staring at me that morphs into Christopher's face. I open my eyes, inhale deeply and look up at Babaji. He nods.

After awhile he says: "The new shrine is coming along nicely. I'm very pleased. And the trail, it's all lovely. Thank you for your hard work." A long pause while he circulates his breath, coral beads moving through his fingers.

"Faith tells me you have business coming up in the next few months where you may see Christopher again." He looks off into the distant valley, then stares directly above me, inhaling sharply. "It's still there, that attachment, the old samsara."

I nod, not knowing what to say; then whispering, "Yes Babaji, it's still there."

"This pattern doesn't serve you. Focus within. Stay away from Christopher if you can. Break the karma. Don't let your inner work go to waste." Then laughing; "Life ain't easy for a girl named Sue."

"I wear my mala everyday and always meditate. It helps," running my fingers along the rosewood beads.

"You're a serious student. I see that. You're doing well," Babaji says to me, his voice low, almost a whisper. "Maybe you should think about moving into the ashram, becoming one of my teachers."

He looks up over my head again, circulates his breath. "You've been initiated by Nityananda, this is your lineage. You belong here," he says sweetly.

"Wow," is all I can say. Then, "Thank you Babaji. I'll think about this. I love you and I'm grateful for everything you've given me."

He smiles, then takes the coral mala from his lap and lifts it over my head, placing it gently around my neck. "This was a gift to me long ago from my teacher. It will keep you safe when you see Christopher, when you struggle with samsaras."

Then waving me off: "Meditate, love Nityananda, you'll be fine." He rises to walk inside, briefly patting the top of my head, sending Shakti through my toes, the coral mala hot against my neck. An image appears of Nityananda sitting where Babaji just sat. The energy swirls down my spine leaving me elated.

I sit on the deck long after Babaji walks inside, watching a thin moon climb above the tall trees, still soaking up the grace, fingers running along the new coral beads, warm with Shakti. The image of Nityananda still lingers on Babaji's chair until I rise to find my way through the bramble, down to the road; my mind spinning in the shadowy light.

On the long walk down the road to my car, John corners me, asks for a ride into town. I'm amused, watching our interaction from a distance, feeling stirred by it and at the same time removed, observing and resisting. On the winding drive to Boulder we share stories of Alabama, the beaches where our families rented vacation homes, the stark beauty of Sand Island, the thrill of catching mackerel with our dads.

When we get to town I pull over at the street corner where he wants to be dropped off. Without asking, he leans in and kisses me in a way that reminds me of Christopher, deep and sensitive, over the edge. He looks exactly like Christopher then; his blue eyes merging with Christopher's in my memory. I'm deeply drawn in, attracted and repulsed; aware of the pattern Babaji just spoke about.

Eventually I push him away but my hands are shaking, my body trembling as he opens the door and gets out, looking back to blow a kiss my way, back pack slung over his shoulder as he turns to go.

Later, walking into my apartment, I catch the tail end of the phone ringing. Checking my missed calls, I see that it was Christopher, our souls still lingering in the spark, our old connection channeling through this 21-year-old hitchhiker. It rips the scab from the wound to know we're still connected.

I remember the coral mala around my neck, reach up to grab it, the warm beads comforting as I sit in front of Nityananda's altar basking in the Shakti that still surges through the smooth stones; giving me a tingly rush from the top of my head down to my toes.

A few days later, there's a knock on my door and I surrender to John O'Malley, disappointed in myself, overcome with longing, wasting the accumulated Shakti, trembling in the moment of passion.

II

THE ROSE GARDEN

New Orleans, Louisiana – Summer 1992

"Sue, I met a Shaman," says Gordon grinning, sitting down across from me, black hair several inches longer, loose and wild around his face with a hint of a ponytail. He leans back in the chair, hands folded behind his head.

Gordon is wild and terrifying, brilliant and unaware; he's here to tweak our navigation before leaving for another wild place; I admire his clarity, his business mind, his ability to drop between worlds; how I wish I could climb out of these trenches myself, rise above the drone of deadlines, drudgery, stay above the mundane and yet pay the rent. Who would I be then? What would I look like? What would the world look like from there and how would I find my way?

"Tell me everything," I say giggling, leaning forward over the pages of galley copy spread across my desk; our latest issue laid out page by page.

"We were in the Amazon visiting a friend," he chuckles like a young boy, "We flew over the jungle in a twin engine bush plane. Marion was terrified but I loved it," grinning wide. "When we landed, the runway was muddy, middle of nowhere, we slid right off the end," laughing again, "So much happened, Sue, it's hard to explain."

He describes a chance meeting with a holy man, a sacred ritual, hallucinogens; "Too many impossible things," he smiles looking away into the distance. He shakes his head, eyes bright and clear; he seems different, cleansed or healed in some way.

"I understand about impossible things," I say when he's finished his story.

"I know you do. Are you still going to your ashram?" he asks focusing on me. I nod and share a few stories that make him smile. He asks briefly if I've seen Christopher, looking kind and sweet when I tell him I haven't but still think about him.

Then leaning in, tapping his fingers on the desk, "Listen, this pending supplement legislation; it's a huge deal. I want you to fly to New Orleans for the food technology conference. That guy Kessler, head of the FDA is giving a keynote. Find out what he thinks of the legislation." Sitting up straight in his chair, all businessy now: "Lots of my friends, company owners, are really upset about this. We need to cover it for the magazine. Stay on top of it. It's important," then standing up, starting to leave, turning back and nodding, "You're doing a great job, Sue. Keep it up." He's quickly out the door, my head still reeling from his impossible stories.

We'd been covering this pending legislation for months; writing call-to-action blurbs, requesting that readers write letters to congress supporting their right to buy vitamins and herbs that don't undergo the billions of dollars of research that only pharmaceutical companies can afford; most of our industry's science as valid as theirs, but without the funding only available to large drug companies.

As my herbalist friend Chris Hobbs once explained; anyone can grow mint in their garden and use it for stomach ailments and the FDA doesn't like that. If everyone grew cancer remedies in their back yard the pharmaceutical industry would go out of business tomorrow.

Hopefully now with Gordon's support, I'll get the budget we need to actually cover the story, fly in to interview Kessler, find out what other food industries think. A quick phone call to Margaret and its all approved; a hefty addition to our travel budget.

Later that day, meeting with staff, we plan the trip; phone calls are made, emails sent and eventually we're promised a few minutes back stage with Kessler after his keynote. I'm thrilled that two of my best writers are going. They've never been to New Orleans.

A week later we land in the muggy familiar of New Orleans; Laurel and Gloria appalled at the heat, profusely sweaty in their fine silk dresses. I'm comforted by the dense summer air, flooded with memories of my grandpa, seductive and painful, as we walk the narrow cobbled streets of the French Quarter, take the ferry, once his ferry, across the Mississippi to Algiers and back again.

In the hotel room, I prop a small framed photo of Nityananda, hands large and luminous, on my bedside table, waking early to meditate in front of it, delighted to say "yes" when a housekeeper asks if he's one of my relatives.

On the crowded sidewalks of Dumaine, Canal, Chartres, as we hurry to events, I try to share stories of my dad's house in Algiers, my childhood on Canal Boulevard, summers in Long Beach and the hurricane; but it's all too much to tell, overwhelms me to remember it even though Laurel and Gloria are encouraging, happy to listen and glad I'm no longer talking about Christopher.

In the evenings we visit my favorite restaurants; eating Beef Brisket with Creole Horseradish at Tujaque's (pointing out the table where my parents sat for their first date); and Shrimp Etouffee at Galatoires (where Ralph O'Malley, man of the river, was an honored guest) and later in the evening settling into the sugar-powdered tables of Café Du Monde for Café Au Lait and beignets.

By day we attend the food technology convention; strolling aisles and aisles of new product booths, vendors pitching their technological approach to nutrition, pushing new food samples into our hands. I'm appalled when a man behind a well-stocked booth, busily talking to grocery store owners from Safeway and King Soopers, reaches out to offer us a taste of his completely synthetic ketchup: "There's absolutely no tomato in it at all," he beams proudly, "It tastes just like ketchup!"

I smile politely and ask him why this is a good thing. He looks at me like I'm a child, nodding his head, slowing his words: "We need to feed the world, have food supplies that we can ship everywhere to stop hunger, food that never perishes," he explains all of this carefully, patient with my ignorance.

"But it isn't really food then is it?" I ask, trying to sound innocent about this topic that I care so deeply about. "There's no nutrition, really, is there?"

He laughs warmly and explains: "Of course there is (silly girl). We infuse it with synthetic compounds of vitamins and proteins."

"Thank you for your time, thank you," we say in unison, backing away from the booth, Gloria getting his name and information; asking if we can quote him in a story.

Attending seminars, taking notes, gathering hand-outs, learning more about their philosophy of feeding the world through the wonders of synthetic foods, I feel homesick for our people; our aisles of natural products, unprocessed foods, herbal remedies; I miss the tofu makers, herbalists and organic gardeners.

At each event I ask the speakers if they have any long-term research studies on the effects of purely synthetic foods on human health, on our immune systems; asking point blank at one seminar if they've explored possible links between soaring cancer rates and processed foods. No one seems to understand my question.

My stomach turns at lunch in their cafeteria as I read their menu of prepared synthetic foods; remembering the pain of Paul and Crissie's early deaths; knowing in my bones that our bodies need fresh unprocessed foods, vibrant living things straight from the garden; that somehow these simple foods put us in alignment with life. I try not to be angry at this world.

Later that evening, we get our press passes for Kessler's keynote and take seats in the front. He appears on stage addressing the vast audience humbly and intelligently. I like him right away. He reiterates the FDAs job to oversight all areas of food and supplement development; even this industry, he cautions them.

I'm surprised to like him, to realize he's quite brilliant; though he appears tired, overworked, pressured from all sides, caught in the middle of opposing million dollar industries. Yet he also seems deeply aware of the game and somehow honest in the midst of the chaos.

We meet afterwards backstage. Gloria and Laurel have their notebooks and recorders, ask intelligent questions which he ponders thoughtfully, gives surprising answers to; reveals without revealing that supplements will be regulated as always but never banned as certain groups are lobbying for. "I'm deeply aware of the opposing financial interests," he says kindly near the end, graciously shaking our hands as he slips out the back door with his entourage, headed for his private flight back to Washington.

That night we stay up late in our rooms, discussing his keynote, his answers to our questions, the soggy heat making our bodies heavy, our voices droopy. Laurel, a musician, surprises us with her lilting operatic voice from the shower singing Life is a Cabaret; Gloria and I rolling on our beds laughing, sharing stories of our days in the newsroom.

The next morning Laurel and Gloria fly home. I check out of the hotel walking several blocks to Café du Monde where my mom and dad sit waiting; dad gets up to give me a hug, teary eyed and sentimental.

Our plan is to have lunch with my mom's sisters at Aunt Ruby's house. None of us have seen mom's family in years. This sudden reunion came as a surprise; planned by Ruby when mom mentioned in a rare phone call that she and dad were driving to New Orleans to pick me up from a business trip.

Dad with his infallible memory for directions drives us straight to Aunt Ruby's house tucked somewhere north of Algiers, through neighborhoods that seem dimly familiar, beneath the interstate, homes butting up against each other, slim front yards jumbled with stone carvings of Virgin Mary, her hands in prayer, and Jesus with his arms spread wide; silver chain link fences tall and foreboding around every home.

Inside it smells of corn bread and red beans. "Oh Sue Ellen, Sue Ellen," coos Aunt Ruby; her enormous eyes dark and brown like mine dominating her tiny face, her hair glistening black and piled high on top of her head. She wraps her arms tight around me, then pushes me back so she can study my face, "Oh you're such a beautiful girl! You always were! It's been too long," tears in her eyes as she ushers me into the kitchen for iced tea. Her daughter, my cousin M'liss, rises from a chair where she's feeding one of her children to offer me a hug, both of us awkward after not seeing each other for twenty years or more.

More sisters arrive, Hilda, Elaine, Delta, all so familiar from long ago, their voices melodious with laughter, then yelling and talking over each other, childhood habits resurfacing; my mom's voice rising above them all to take center stage, parading my elegant dad through this house of noisy women.

M'liss and I sit in the kitchen catching up. She's been married to her childhood sweetheart for twenty years. They have a jumble of kids, most of them swinging on a play-set in the back yard; she points out the window to show me. She works as a dental hygienist; tells me she hates her job but it pays the bills; her mouth a tight frown, asking in wonderment how I got a job like mine, so foreign to her she says sweetly, studying my long flowy rayon dress.

"I envy you," she says, rolling her eyes when her youngest whines and demands more soda.

"But you have everything," I tell her. "Look at these gorgeous children and a man you've loved forever. I envy you. I've always wanted a family."

"I'm sorry about your husband dying. Must have been tough. Heard a little about it from mom," she says taking my hand; the years unraveling back through time to the night we sat together in her living room to watch the Beatles first appearance on Ed Sullivan; both of us screaming and crying with elation, our lives changing in surprising ways.

"Everybody goes through tough things," I say.

"Right," she says smiling, looking at me gratefully, urging her daughter to go outside and play with her siblings.

Around the crowded dinner table I listen to their stories; "Remember how the phone would ring and Ruby would announce who was calling before we answered? And she was always right!" Hilda's voice rising to a shout to be heard above her sisters. "Yes, yes, and remember when Shirley came home from a high school dance and said she'd seen the man she was going to marry?" interjects Elaine, "She hadn't even spoken to him yet! She just saw Tommy across the room and knew! Oh he was the catch," she coos, grinning over at my dad who smiles and laughs, "Nawww," he says humbly, "She was the catch," putting his hand on top of mom's at the table. "But she was right," adds Ruby, "She was always right," looking at my mom, raising a glass of iced tea to toast them.

These women are witches, they know things, see into crevices, follow whispers; they're crazy, schizophrenic, alcoholic, suicidal, divorced; they're gifted, incredibly wise, too sensitive, impoverished, struggling, unable to find a good man; their eyes overly large and expressive for their tiny perfectly boned faces; their voices a rising chorus of competing arias; a crescendo of dueling sopranos; they're lost and subdued, surrendered to the drudgeries of daily life, completely unsure of themselves. I am just like them.

"You have the gift too Sue Ellen," chimes in Aunt Ruby, "You always did honey. Hilda do you remember when Sue was little and we would babysit, roll her hair, give her perms, the things she would say about the future, so strange from such a young child, all turned out to be true." They all nod in agreement, M'liss rolling her eyes and whispering; "Oh their stories, Sue, you just never know," both of us laughing.

My father is the coveted prize at the table, tall and elegant in his business suit, laughing gracefully with the women, all of them fussing around him; bringing more food, pouring iced tea, asking questions about his business, his family. He's easy and gracious; engaging in their stories, making them laugh. Mom, beaming with pride, never leaves his side.

It's clear that my mom, the youngest, was the star of this line-up; her voice even now rising commandingly above the others, charming and lilting her way through a story; most of her sisters widowed, divorced, supporting families from garages transformed into beauty salons; her marriage to dad an impossible fairy tale come true.

I'm startled by my striking resemblance to her sisters; I have the same eyes as Ruby, Elaine's smile, Hilda's nose. Yet overall, I look most like Elaine, the sister just a year older than mom; "The pretty one with the most troubled life," as my mom frequently described her; married to an alcoholic, struggling with addictions, illnesses, financial ruin.

All throughout my childhood mom called me Elaine; a slip of the tongue she would say, sometimes admitting how nasty Elaine had been to her; how they competed for men, even competed for my dad's attention on his first visit to their house to see mom. She'd almost named me after this sister whom she'd never liked; their love-hate relationship a kind of foreboding prophecy.

As the day winds down, we say our good-byes with tears, hugs, and promises to keep in touch. Dad navigates us in his town car back through the narrow neighborhoods and up the interstate ramp for the eastward drive to Mobile; surprising us later when he turns off the interstate to head south towards Long Beach, pulls up to the empty lot in the watery light of sunset. "We'll be right back Shirley," he says to mom motioning for me to come with him. "Sue Ellen don't ruin your nice shoes in that mess," mom cautions from the window as we tiptoe through the overgrown bushes and rock-a-chaws to touch the water oak still standing at the top of the yard.

I lean into it, inhale its old familiar musky scent, "It still smells like our Long Beach," I say. But dad has already turned away and walked deep into the overgrowth that covers the land where our houses stood; surveying the ground where he once found Grandpa's rusted wrench, then quickly wiping at his eyes.

His shoulders are slumped; he looks forlorn and old, his gaze rising up to follow the dead branches of our second water oak, the one beside the driveway that towered over our house; then looking back towards the creek that ran behind the tool shed; then turning back to face me, hands in his pockets, lips tight, looking lost.

I climb through the brush, holding up my rayon dress. "Dad," I whisper, standing next to him. "It's too sad. We have to move on; it's nearly 20 years," I look into his eyes, pleading, resisting the overwhelming melancholy.

"Dad it's time to sell the land," I say, knowing that he and his brothers discuss this every year; always agreeing that land values are too low, despising the condo developers who've already bought most of these coastal properties.

"Dad I've been doing some therapy work, or maybe not therapy, I have a kind of meditation teacher," I stammer on, not sure how to talk about Babaji. "Anyway," clearing my throat, "He's helping me heal some of my grief. A lot of it is from Long Beach, from what happened to us here. And well, maybe, it's not such a good idea for us to keep coming back here, for you to keep grieving this." He's not listening now, bending down to find a remnant from the oyster shell driveway, buried beneath a broken pine branch.

"Dad maybe we could buy a new beach house or something." My voice trails off, the idea feeling as hollow as it sounds, both of us knowing Long Beach wasn't a beach house; it was some kind of paradise lost, an unattainable nirvana. Our mystical memories of wild and happy cousins, sugar cane fields, oyster shell driveways, water oaks, fresh spring water bubbling up from sandbars; all of it seems like a fantasy in the retelling; each moment fading just as we grab hold, nothing left but empty land, an unbearable story that still haunts my dreams.

"C'mon dad," I say again, tugging at his arm, "Let's go home." The drive back is quiet, sad, like every drive away from Long Beach.

Later that night in bed in the Mobile house, I rise and fall from sleep, burdened with dreams of New Orleans, Long Beach; a dinner table full of women who all have the same dark eyes as mine; the mystery of my mother's voice, brassy and effervescent in a crowded room.

I'm kneeling in church, realize it's the St Thomas Church next door to Long Beach; its front doors swung wide open to the rolling waves of the Mississippi Sound. I feel afraid, like something awful is about to happen, try to get up, walk back to our house, to the Water Oak, but my legs won't move, they don't work right. The rotating fans inside the church rustle papers in the pews around me, and looking up at the altar I'm taken aback with the beauty of Mother Mary hovering in front, her blue robes swaying in the breeze that now rolls in from the doors, her hands clasped in prayer; a sea of human voices echoing around me, a cacophony of prayer as the wall of water rolls in heavy and determined through the church doorway.

I wake up sweating, trying to open the bedroom windows that won't open; the air conditioner loud and whiny through my bedroom vent, still there's no oxygen reaching my lungs, nothing to prevent suffocation in the heaviness of sea level; my high-altitude lungs unable to acclimatize to the weight of dreams, still feeling that losing Long Beach is my fault, that I could've done better, stood up to the waves, saved us all.

The next morning, mom wakes me early; we'd planned to spend the day together visiting her favorite place – Bellingrath Gardens just south of Mobile along Fowl River. We need to get there as soon as it opens at 8 a.m. to avoid the afternoon heat, she reminds me, knocking lightly on my bedroom door as I struggle up from the night.

We sit in her kitchen eating cold cereal and the local bakery's doughy biscuits that she heats in the oven for me; today they make me gag; both of us nervous and uncomfortable to imagine spending an entire day alone together.

My dad, dressed in his suit and tie for work, hurries into the kitchen, grabs his coffee, taps his foot on the floor nervously while he eats biscuits and draws us a map for our drive to the gardens.

"I dreamed about Long Beach," I tell him.

He nods, "Me too," he says looking down at his biscuits. No one speaks for awhile, then dad stands up, kisses my head, says: "You all better get going before the day heats up." He puts his dishes in the dishwasher, lingers in the kitchen doorway looking worried; "You girls have fun," he says trying to look cheerful.

After a long drive along the winding river road just south of Mobile, the day is already warming when we park the car at the entrance of Bellingrath. We get in line behind a small gathering of mostly women. "Do we want tickets for the home and gardens or just the gardens?" asks mom, looking worried, a jumble of emotions creasing her face.

"Let's do both," I say, acting more excited than I feel. "Can't remember the last time we spent an entire day together, mom, just the two of us. Let's enjoy it." She buys the tickets, turns to hand me my map of the gardens, perspiration already dotting her upper lip.

A pungent blend of salt marsh and roses greet us as we enter, pulling us down the walkway. "Wow," I say, pausing inside the entrance. "I forgot how beautiful this was."

"Oh I know, I haven't been here in years either honey. Your dad and I used to make the visit every spring."

We agree to start at the Rose Garden, both of us seduced by its dizzy jumble of colors in the early sun; lipstick red, lemon yellow, cool-aid coral creating shimmery splotches that rise in the heat like a visual disruption, a wavy migraine against the horizon. As we move closer the colors take shape as petals, leaves, and specie names written on white cards poking up from everywhere.

"Oh mom, smell this," I say bending down to inhale a deep pink rose that leaves me drunk, stupored with delight; mom looks over at me giggling, youthful, equally altered. For a brief second we are sisters and I am older, admiring her spark, jealous of her charms, the way she laughs so easily, her voice drifting above the roses like perfume, a scent of joy - refreshing in the heavy air; I feel protective and sorry; she's delicate and tough. She's as bruised as the rose petals fallen on the sidewalk. I've stepped on her, all over her.

We keep stooping to smell, pausing in the ridiculous happiness of rose after rose after rose spread out jubilantly, defiantly, in the warm sun; their enchantment winding us all the way down the brick path to the eucalyptus trees waving along the river. We bend over repeatedly to take notice of small things, read cards and names, compare scents and shapes; our words gladly, ecstatically, youthfully, gratefully jumbled; we're thrilled to inhale the scent of forgiveness.

"Mom, I love roses. I could just sit here and be happy forever."

"Oh I know Sue, I know. Grandpa could grow roses better than anyone. He filled our yard at Long Beach with them. Do you remember? He brought me some to plant in Mobile, but they never really bloomed for me."

Later we sit side-by-side on the edge of the roses under a white-lattice pagoda, listening to the bubbling of a fountain nearby. "This is wonderful, mom."

"It is, Sue, so happy we came here," she smiles, opening her purse to pull out a Kleenex, using it to dab at the perspiration above her lip, then handing me one.

"Where should we go next?"

"Oh to the Asian gardens," she gushes, "That's my favorite spot," pointing out its location on the map. We find our way past the gazebo garden, its tall red spikes of spiral ginger dazzling in the morning light like a dream interrupted.

"Look mom, this is my favorite herb, ginger. I take it to calm my stomach. Look how beautiful the blooms are."

"I know honey, I love them too. I've got ginger growing in my garden at home. I'll show you when we get back." Then looking at me, "Do you still have that nervous stomach? You had that when you were little."

"A little bit mom. Not too bad."

"You know I always had that too when I was young. But I outgrew it. Thought you would too."

I nod, feeling relieved and glad to find common ground, the talk flowing easily. Strolling through the Asian gardens, we gush at the trailing yellow blooms of jasmine, cascading mums, gingko flowers. She's thrilled by the simplicity of the Asian-inspired landscape; its stunning array of pagodas, arched bridges, pendulous vines, winding walkways; "Oh Sue I love this so much," she says sitting down on a bench beneath a Japanese trellis. "It's so peaceful here. Wish I had a garden like this," she says wistfully.

"But you sorta have a room like this, right mom? Your Chinese-inspired living room."

"Yes I do," she laughs. "Must be my past lifetime as a Buddhist like you say," she smiles at me, her voice sparkly as a silver bell - as dad once called it.

After awhile we move to the great lawn with its carpet of blooming flowers; purple coneflower, black-eyed Susans, Russian Sage; we follow a winding path of succulents through a hillside rock garden, mom knowing the names of each plant - familiar from her succulent garden alongside our patio.

"Mom you should have been a garden planner or a master gardener. You know so much about these plants and your yard is amazing," I say dabbing at the drops of perspiration on my face, the humidity thick and annoying, sneaking up on us whenever we sit.

"Oh I've always loved plants, Sue," she says, excited to talk about her azaleas, camellias, wisteria vines, magnolia trees and the precious blue Hydrangea bush that Grandpa brought her from Long Beach years ago. She tells me that the neighbors ask for her advice when they plant their gardens, plan their yards. "I just never felt like I knew enough about gardening to make it my career."

Later, sitting by the pools in the Live Oak terraces, it feels like sitting in a dream; I close my eyes and lean back against the bench. "Mom did you enjoy seeing your sisters in New Orleans?"

"Oh yes, it's always so good to see Ruby. Did I tell you she's reading War and Peace?"

"I love that. Yeah, she's pretty amazing. It was great to see my cousin M'liss. Do you miss your family?"

"Oh I don't know Sue, yes and no." She pauses, studying the trailing purple blooms cascading wild and lovely from a nearby balcony. "I was never that close to my sisters; mainly just Ruby. The others were so much older and kinda loud, hard to be around. But Ruby, Elaine, we were closer."

"You were close to Elaine?"

"Well, she was just a little older than me so I spent more time with her. It's hard to remember, so long ago."

"You've told me many times that I remind you of her."

"Well, Elaine was beautiful, all the boys wanted to date her. Once when dad came to the door, Elaine hid behind the screen and flirted with him, pretended to be me," her voice incredulous, annoyed, shaking her head.

"How do I remind you of her, mom?"

133

"You always had boyfriends coming around the house; you're beautiful like her."

"But you didn't like Elaine, mom. I'm not really like her, am I?"

"I don't know Sue Ellen; it was so many years ago," she gets up, wants to keep walking. "Let's get out of this heat, visit the mansion, have some iced tea," she says.

We walk into the meticulously restored antebellum home; it's enormous dining room set with flowered china and gold-rimmed crystal, large porcelain vases lining the fireplace mantel. As we walk upstairs to see the bedrooms, mom walks closely behind me on the grand front stairway; "I don't want anyone to see up your dress," she whispers as we climb. My dress is knee-length. But she's sweet, protective. I cherish the moment; smile and say "thank you mom."

Later in the café sipping iced tea I say; "Mom tell me more about your dad. He was an herbalist right?"

"He was a good man, Sue. By the time I was born he was pretty old, though. I didn't really know him as well as my siblings did. I was the only one born in the city you know. We'd moved into town by then, away from the farm because he'd gotten sick, some kind of infection from the cows or something. We'd moved to town because of his health."

Her voice trails off. "But yes, he'd make a poultice if you had a headache, or a tea. He always had mint tea on the stove." Then looking up at me, "I didn't really like the way those things smelled," she smiles. "I guess I was more of a modern girl, you know, the youngest."

"Yeah, that makes sense."

"But he was very kind, very sweet. It was my mother who was strict with us. Guess she had to be with so many kids."

"What do you remember most?"

"Oh, I don't know. Our house was always a mess, noisy, crowded, everyone talking at once, relatives visiting day and night, arguing at the kitchen table. I don't know Sue. I just wanted to get out, live on my own as soon as I could."

Later when I ask about her older brothers, she tells me that her favorite was Blaise, the sweet one, named after their father. "He died suddenly when he came back from the war," she says looking out the window at the distant river winding through the waving ginkgo trees. "But I don't remember much from back then, Sue, it was all a long time ago." She looks at me, takes my hand, "Sue you know I've always loved you. You were my first-born, very special. I hope you know that."

"I do mom. I have great memories from our years in New Orleans - before we moved to Mobile."

"Those were the best years," she sighs. "You were so well-behaved, even when you were little. I'd dress you in a nice organza dress, patent-leather shoes; we'd wear hats and gloves, take the streetcar into the city, go shopping at Maison Blanche, have lunch at the counter. You loved the nice places – Gallatoire's, Tujaques." She laughs, looks at me and shakes her head, "We really had fun."

"I can kind of remember that."

"But when Roy was born and then Micky, and of course we moved, none of it was the same anymore. I couldn't take the boys places. Life was different in Mobile."

I sit listening, like a well-behaved child, longing for those lost moments in New Orleans, just the two of us happy on a streetcar.

"Mobile was so small, so disappointing," she says, suddenly looking tired, her voice fading as we get up from the table and head out into the heat of the July afternoon.

That night in my childhood bedroom at the Mobile house, I float out through the wooden shutters, up into the tops of the tall pines where I'm sitting on a curb in New Orleans beside my mom. We're at a street corner; a sign says Dufrene and points to the right towards a busy part of town crowded with streetcars and people hurrying along the sidewalks. I look over at mom and realize she's in her 20s, more beautiful than I remembered.

She turns to face me and says something; her voice kind and loving. It stirs a longing for something essential, for that necessary thing, for a piece of her I never knew. I ask; "Mom did you love living here? It's such a busy city with so many people. Were you ever scared?"

"I loved it here," she says. "This was home. I loved these tall buildings, the sound of the ships coming down the river, the

SUE FREDERICK

evenings we spent in the quarter with our friends; your dad and I, this was our world."

She says all of this in a tone I'm not familiar with; it's young and undamaged. Her voice is unconditional, all-knowing, forgiving; I let the sound of it wash over me, erasing everything; I've never disappointed her; she's never wounded me.

She takes my hand and we walk through the busy streets; she guides me through familiar neighborhoods pointing out buildings that she loved, places she often went; her voice lilting into the French creole cadence of her childhood.

We're standing in front of her childhood home in Gretna, a jumble of dimly recognizable people lined along the railing of the narrow porch. Her sister Ruby steps forward, waves, is happy to see us. My Grandpa Dufrene emerges from the garden beside the house holding a branch of sugar cane. He slices it with a knife and offers us a taste of the sugar that oozes from the cane. This is God's nectar, he says in his heavily accented French creole voice.

I remember how much I've missed him; how he died when I was twelve and I cried for days, my parents unable to understand why I grieved so much for a grandpa I rarely saw; no one fully grasping the way he offered kindness so readily; helped me feel worthy when I was doubting; always got up from the kitchen table to take me outside to the garden the moment I arrived in his crowded noisy home; knowing that I needed the quiet earth, the canopy of plants, to smell the sugar cane, weed the tomatoes, feel the sun on my head; and that mom would soon call me from the kitchen to help with dinner and that would be the last place I would ever want to go. He knew things.

I look at mom; she's transformed now into a truly exquisite beauty, someone unknown to me; yet it's still her. "I loved you so much, Sue Ellen," she says, suddenly sad, apologetic. "I never meant for things to go the way they did." I comfort her; wrap my arms around her. "It's okay mom. It's really all okay."

The next day at breakfast I'm reminded of her damage; how her mind gets hung up on the smallest most irrelevant details, a word the neighbor said carelessly years ago that sticks to her like super glue, the thing I mentioned last summer over dinner that she has festered over ever since; the tiniest speck of food left in her

136

stainless kitchen sink this morning that I deliberately slovenly purposefully inconsiderately left to torture her, to keep her up at night, to destroy the stainlessness of steel, spoil all future meal preparation for generations to come, for centuries really; these things never to be forgotten, forgiven, unleashed, absolved no matter their intent, no matter the transgressor, but especially by me the sacred and chosen eldest of her children; the one who never lived up to stainless steel perfection, the flawless finish she demanded; I will simply step away from the kitchen.

Back in Boulder, I unpack and change clothes, eager for a late afternoon hike up Sanitas. An hour later I'm alone in my favorite spot near the summit facing west, the sun-warmed boulders soothing on my back.

Pulling out the coral mala, I'm desperate to close my eyes and meditate, get some clarity, shake the never-ending sadness; but less than five minutes in, the grief erupts like a tidal wave and I'm sobbing out loud.

I miss my dad already, haunted as always by the way he says good-bye at the airport, his lips tight and quivering, his eyes blue and moist. The brief visit to Long Beach still replaying in my brain like a song I can't shake.

Why, I ask Nityananda, is it so painful to go home and painful to come back? Why do I long to stay there with dad; the two of us building a beach house in the soggy air, no a bay house, high on the bluff, safe from the hurricanes, above the mosquitos; he'll have a fishing shed and his private boat dock far below on the calm waters; we'll pull up crab nets for dinner in the evening and cast into the bay for mackerel for breakfast, both of us tanned and happy with our simple lives, praying at night to the moon, holding our hands up into the perpetual light that shines through our windows; I'll write best-selling novels to support us, he won't have to work, he'll just be happy and simple the way he is, the way he was; it'll be better than Long Beach; we'll laugh crazily at night on the porch about how better the view is here than it was in Mississippi way back then and what the heck were we thinking, why didn't we escape sooner, build this long before Camille was named, became a torment on the weather map; why didn't we realize that Long Beach was a thing we could have again, elsewhere, anywhere, here, now, why didn't we, why didn't we.

I cry like a lost girl, climbing back through the brambles of Long Beach, leaning against the water oak, swimming with long lazy strokes towards Cat Island. I'll move back home next month, buy a beach condo, pack up everything here, give it away; this is all a disaster anyway, a useless cause, a feeble attempt to live a bold life that became a tragedy instead; my mother was right, who do I think I am?

Take this away, take me away, I beg to the emptiness, is anyone really there anyway; giving up and laying down flattened on the rocks; nothing between me and heaven, just the void of my unworthiness staring back.

I float up gladly into the void, release my tense grip on the earth, sit at Babaji's feet again as he pounds on my head, laughing and repeating what he's said before; but I never listen do I, I just never listen; will I listen this time as he tells me to release the past; that it's just an old samsara, a family pattern of sadness that I need to break. He is so right, of course he is, but I am drowning and everyone else is correct, right about all of it, aware that I'm a loser way down deep and always will be, and why do I keep trying so hard not to be?

I decide to stay on these rocks as the light fades into chilly evening; I want the vultures to find me; to become dinner for the coyotes and mountain lions; transform my grief into something life-giving, fertilizer for what comes next.

Nityananda takes my hand, something he's never done before; his hands are gigantic, like a cartoon character's oversized limbs, his tallness defying imagination as he sits beside me, gentle as a bear. You have to want to break this, he says kindly, though it's not in words, can't explain it, how it comes in pure as light, unquestionably true, something I've always known; that I have to want to break the pattern not for myself but for the others. Yes - he nods in approval, his hand so large and hot around mine; like a fever holding me, then a sudden release and he's not there anymore, just a blur of color, a disturbance in the atmosphere; you do it, you make the effort for the future, for what comes after you, for the others coming next in the lineup. You are the fertilizer.

Burn it all up into dust, ashes, compost. That thought jolts me upright, like someone just yelled a ridiculously loud command directly into my ear.

I sit staring at the continental divide, the shifting tectonic plates in the distance, absorbing the last of the high-altitude sun as it settles for the night, letting the thin air alter me, knowing that I've been given so much and have been ungrateful. Truly ungrateful.

What will I do with all this wisdom from Babaji and Nityananda, the gifts buried in my pain and losses? What exactly are these gifts? How do I use them in this world to get by, to rise above, to pay what's owed, to thrive?

A thought comes sliding through, riding in on the orange glow of the evening sun; I need to break this sadness for my dad's benefit, he's too broken by disappointments to do it himself; if I can break the pattern for myself, churn it into compost, the new life giving energy that emerges will lift him above his grief and disappointments. But I can only break it from here, not there, not in a beach house, or on a bay dock where I'll slip into reminiscing, call out to the water oaks from my dreams, attempt to swim to Cat Island all the while knowing I'll never make it.

Or maybe the struggle, the effort is not just for him but for all future generations of our encoded circle; our gene pool; maybe my inner work, my lifting above sorrow can transform family patterns, loosen their dark grip on us.

If this is true then I need to give it another go; jump back into the ring; maybe move into the ashram after all; make a commitment to the work.

But I still can't see it; can't imagine living at Shambhava, sleeping in the crowded bunkroom, filling my days with chores, cleaning duties, meditation classes; never having enough time to do what is essential for me.

So what is the answer? I cry out loud to the vastness. "Just wait," says Nityananda; "Just wait. You'll know."

The sky has fallen suddenly night-ish and a little scary, yet a thin moon rises to the east and as I step out of my hiding place and climb back onto the trail, its glow is like a fine nightlight precisely revealing each step home.

The next day back at New Times, I bury myself in the job; happy to work with my team; craft our next issue, hammer out stories about legislation, Kessler's words; I'm grateful for my deepening connection to Laurel and Gloria.

In the following weeks I'm thrilled to be invited to visit an herbal company in Switzerland, walk their Echinacea fields, see how they make their tinctures. The international flight is long, disorienting, exhilarating – takes me far from my little life in Boulder.

Is everyone in Switzerland beautiful? I ask the company executive as he drives us from Zurich to Alpenzen. He laughs, looking at me kindly, says: "That's how we see Americans."

They take my breath away with their perfect English, German, French, Italian – all spoken within one conversation to whomever asks a question. At the dinner table, their talk is witty and brilliant, their kindness overwhelming.

We walk through lavender fields that intoxicate my senses with happiness, have dinner in cafes where the smell of sour cheese rises pungent from our table, repulsing me, trying not to gag, don't want to hurt their feelings about this cheese they truly love. But I need to step outside for a minute, gagging as I hurry to the door.

Visiting their offices, pristine and sparse, we discuss the future of herbal medicine. I meet their growers, the sweetest family I've ever met, raising their children wild, barefoot and happy amongst the blooming purple Echinacea flowers. This, if I could have this, I pray to Nityananda walking hand in hand with their little girl, blonde haired and perfect, speaking English as well as I do.

I lust after our herbal tour guide, a man who would never leave Switzerland for me, feel happy to flirt with him. It must be my hormones. Do all women long for soul mates and children once they're old enough to worry that it might not happen? I ask Nityananda this question - late at night in my tiny mountain chalet bedroom, mala in my hands, staring at his picture, large hands shimmering in the dim light of the tiny room. Is it just that I need a child? I ask.

I hike the hills outside of Lucerne, ride ferries on their frigid and majestic lakes, gasp at the beauty of sheep grazing every hillside, immaculate homes like pictures from a painting, not a speck of dirt, dust or trash to be found anywhere. I spend a week connecting with herbalists and natural product executives; deciding I will marry all of them, live in Switzerland with a house full of tow-headed little girls, cozy and safe in one of their clean orderly homes with a broom on my porch – to keep all the mess away. That's what I need; a life with no mess; a broom on my sweet porch.

I fly home tired and lonely, jet lagged, spend a Sunday afternoon in bed staring at the limbs of the ancient horse chestnut tree just outside my window, dreams pulling me deep into its enormous cozy branches. I feel disconnected from all that's real and obligatory; how will I ever get out of bed again?

The herbal tour guide from Switzerland steps into my bedroom, takes my hand, gets on one knee, asks me to marry; we'll have a Swiss mountaintop wedding; I'll wear flowers in my hair and run barefoot through the edelweiss; we'll grow old together walk hand-in-hand through lavender fields, harvest purple Echinacea for tinctures; we'll have tow-headed children immediately, this week, and I'll walk them to school each morning; just a short walk to the village center, where I'll teach at the school, English or reading, and every day every hour every minute I'll feel happy beyond all reason with a broom on my front porch and money flowing in hourly, daily, weekly, landing on our rooftop in bundles from nowhere; just write your books, he'll say to me adoringly, just raise our children and write your books.

I fall out of the horse chestnut, land heavily on the bed; exhausted from my endless longings; I must get up, out of bed, oh but, oh but. I'm so disgusted with my ridiculous self.

He would be ordinary after all, the herbal tour guy, just like everyone else; he'd have a secret lover, no he'd get a disease, leave me barefoot and pregnant, our business would fail, I'd lose my passport, never be allowed back home; the Shambhava Center would move somewhere warm like Hawaii; I'd drive for days through the Colorado mountains searching and never find Babaji again. My car would stall out, run out of gas on a lonely dirt road in the middle of a forest. Bears would eat me alive.

I sit on the edge of the bed staring at Nityananda's photo, my body heavier than lead; maybe I'm sick or just tired or sick of me or tired of me. I feel chronically fatigued; permanently disabled, unplugged from reality, swimming in a fever of impossible things.

I make a pot of tea in the kitchen, strong and black; you need to have a long talk with your fine self, Sue, I say out loud to the table. You need to learn to accept ordinary things, quit longing for the extraordinary. Ah ha, I say to myself, sipping my tea, there you have it!

I've never seen men as ordinary things. To me, men are pieces of the divine; something that connects me to somewhere else, somewhere way better than this ordinary, obligatory, drudgery-filled existence. Who would ever choose to be here instead of there?

Paul lifted me into that world once, raised the veil and pulled me in - and oh it was exquisite; light filled, liquidy, lovey, need-free, all-knowing, all connected, indescribable, no words for it. And every day here is nothing compared to there - nor can it ever be - given that all things here are densely ordinary, drudgingly difficult, lonelier than shit, and there's never enough love to go around.

But my dad truly was other-worldy, wasn't he? He found God in summer squalls, in the rhythm of shallow waves, in a sudden moon rising like sunlight above the Water Oak. That's extraordinary isn't it? Wasn't he? Isn't he? The first un-canonized saint in America? He loves me in spite of my endless conditions. *He* has enough love to go around.

But maybe he's ordinary after all, Sue. He could never really survive away from Long Beach could he? He disassembled into something broken and weak when he found himself dressed in a business suit, working in an office, selling boilers and burners to paper mills; or sitting at the kitchen table quietly eating biscuits while mom destroyed us.

But Paul wasn't human was he? He glowed as lovingly and patiently as a saint in the midst of having his intestines ripped apart, his veins torn open, his guts spilled out across the sheets.

Oh, but wasn't he angry too? Didn't he wear a t-shirt when you met him that said; "fuck everything and everybody," and didn't he have a masters in divinity but never do a damn thing with it except print more angry t-shirts and climb more mountains?

Well, yes, technically that's true; but Emilio was truly not human; I'm sure of this. He was a thing of the sea, a thing of exotic other-ness, a medicine man, no, a water spirit. Wait, didn't he abandon his wife and baby in Mexico City to play in Mazatlan and move in with you, Sue, because you asked nothing of him? How heavenly is that? Okay, you win. Maybe.

Well there's still the lovely Christopher, isn't there? We can all agree that he's the authentic dropped straight from heaven fabulously fabulous angel - complete with wings and halo - who took all of our breaths away; sucked the air from the universe with each smile; whenever he entered a room we all fell to our knees didn't we? His face so ridiculously easy and open, his body absurdly relaxed, casually sexy; his entire demeanor outrageously receptive to and expectant of our utter and unwavering adoration. Right?

Well, except for the card trick, the sleight of hand; the lies that went unnoticed until everyone had laid their cards on the table and he had won, always won, the entire pot; the grand jackpot; and we knew somehow that he had cheated us, cheated everyone, everywhere, all the time. Okay yeah, except for that part.

The next afternoon I go see David, my acupuncturist. "My God you're a mess," he says poking needles into my scalp, my earlobes, my neck, up and down my spine, my wrists, my feet; "There's no hope for you," he says burning things on my back, deep smoky resinous herbs that smell like toxic ashes; plugging me into pulsing electrical wires, making little exasperated sounds as he works.

Then he sits on the chair, arms crossed, head tilted, looking at me sprawled across his table like a writhing porcupine; he shakes his head like he always does; like I've arrived in his office as his most impossible specimen of hopelessness, the worst case of everything he's ever seen. "You have so many parts out of whack; I think it's a virus, that's why you have a fever; but also you're just worn down, worn out, twisted up, girl, what have you been doing?"

"Traveling, went to Switzerland."

"And?"

"The usual, you know, longing and lusting."

"And before that?"

"Uh, went to New Orleans on a business trip and then to see my parents in Mobile."

"My God, you do love to torture yourself," he shakes his head. "Every time I get you all fixed up, all your chi unblocked, your energy back in balance, you just end up back in here looking like this." Then getting up, standing over me, his voice serious: "Sue, you need to make some changes, can't keep spinning off in so many different directions like this? You're hurting yourself."

"Yep, that's pretty much what Babaji tells me."

"Yes and there's that. What's going on with that?"

"He wants me to move in."

"Sue..." it's a moan or a groan or a deep complaint; he's a longtime friend, a brother, a magnificent healer, or just another blue-eyed already-taken, it-would-have-been-so-great-to-be-us kinda guy showing up in my life again.

He takes the needles out, unplugs me. I sit up to face him. "Well?"

"You know what I'm going to say."

"Say it."

"You don't belong in an ashram. You have gifts, you're a writer, Sue," then sitting down again, shaking his head. "Have you been seeing that married guy again?"

"No, I promise."

"Sue, what will you do, with everything you are, what will you do; New Times is killing you. You're done with that. If you saw yourself for who you are, you'd be you, quit giving yourself away. You need to stop everything and hit the reset button."

"I think that's called death."

He laughs. I love it when I make him laugh.

Days later, I drive to Shambhava for a three day silent meditation retreat with the Sangha; it's a relief to be in the stillness again, my exhaustion lifting with every meditation; my energy recharging as we wash dishes, sweep the dining hall, chant late into the evenings; my loneliness lifting as I walk tired and senseless back to my cabin each night to dream of elephant-headed deities and six-armed goddesses.

On the afternoon of the third day, as we sit in silence in the sunroom, Babaji asks about my trip home to Mobile. I tell him about the sorrowful visit to Long Beach and that I've realized it's up to me to change the sadness that our family carries.

He listens, closes his eyes in meditation, opens them and says: "No it's up to Nityananda. Give that to him to work on. Just keep surrendering everything to Nityananda." His words feel promising, like a great burden lifted from my shoulders. Neither of us mentions his offer to move in, to become a teacher; it sits unspoken and heavy between us.

12

THE MEETING

Baltimore Maryland – Fall 1992

I fly into Baltimore on a warm afternoon for our natural products expo, still invigorated from the retreat at Shambhava and giddy from meditating on the plane; the Guru Gita reverberating in my head.

At the hotel, waiting in the long line to check in, I'm surrounded by familiar faces; the lobby is a sea of waving vitamin company owners, herbal friends, tofu makers, homeopathic manufacturers. I feel right at home.

A sexy crew of natural food retailers strolls by, briefcases under their arms; Christopher in the midst of them, tall, fair-haired, animated and laughing. I turn away to avoid his gaze, recite mantra, circulate my breath.

I feel protected from the frenzy, removed from the bustle; peaceful with Babaji's coral mala warm against my neck; it pulls me high above these mundane conversations.

My friend and neighbor Joseph has told me to set an intention for expo so I don't lose my focus, become scattered, give myself away. I have one; to conduct successful meetings, moderate seminars, attend all events while using mantra, breath and meditation to feel more connected to the divine than the mundane.

Is it true that life happens while we're making other plans; that God laughs at our carefully laid out intentions?

While still waiting in line to check in, a tall man turns around to survey the crowd; his glance lands on me. His eyes are the color of cinnamon, his scent thick with testosterone. We've met before. I'm Thomas, he says, introducing himself. He's from the industry, an herbalist working for an herbal company in California. But I don't know him well. "Will you have dinner?" he asks. "Of course," I answer so quickly it surprises me. My senses are heightened just from standing near him; his hair so soft and brown I want to reach out and touch it, caress his sweet, sensitive face. He's dangerous. I am unstoppably hopeless around men, a jellyfish in front of sharks; a lamb jumping on the sacrificial altar. Or none of those things; I'm just following my intuition, trusting my heart, staying open. Or, as David says, giving myself away. Or this is my soul mate, at last, at last; he's been waiting for me in this line for lifetimes and we'll be married by midnight carried high on the shoulders of our celebrating friends here at expo; all gleefully honoring the arrival of true love, once and for all, the greatest loving couple ever; this spontaneous combustion of a meeting enough to impregnate me immediately; we'll have children by Sunday. Or none of those things.

Later that evening, we take the water taxi, lights shimmering along the shores, holding hands on the bench, watching currents swirl around the bow. I don't know why he takes my hand or why it feels right that he does.

"This river reminds me of my childhood on the Mississippi," I say.

"Oh, hmmm," he nods, not asking about my childhood, not seeming to want to know anything really about me and when I share things about myself anyway he's indifferent, unresponsive; so different from Christopher who cared about every moment from my past, savored each New Orleans memory.

I decide to like it that Thomas doesn't care. I'm here to forget the past, surrender it all to Nityananda, focus on the future; easy to do with Thomas.

I ask him about growing up in Iowa. "Not much to say about Iowa," is his response.

He brings me to an expensive cafe on the far shore, a long way from the convention center; he's reserved and elegant, taller than anyone, gentlemanly and awkward, sweet and silly, complicated and smart. He orders for me and it's just what I wanted; crab cakes and Caesar Salad.

"You're single?" I ask as he pours the wine.

"Oh yes, quite single. Never married."

Over dessert and coffee, the conversation gets easier, starts flowing; I want to know more about him and ask for his birthdate. I give readings to friends about their birth paths, why they're here, what they came to accomplish, I say, laughing as I say it, dismissing it with my tone, making it trivial. Okay, he agrees, let's see what it says.

Looking at his numbers, I explain that he's here to learn about power, how to use it generously, not abusively, instead to empower others, to become an entrepreneur, and that he'll be quite wealthy someday.

Hmmm, doesn't sound like me, he says.

Later, we walk along the riverbank sharing stories; he tells me about a mystical Spanish woman who once broke his heart, but now he thinks she was "truly crazy." He tried to have her committed after they broke up. My stomach turns to hear it; something wrong about the story; about the careful unraveling of a powerful woman.

Again when I ask about his parents or siblings he won't discuss his childhood; "Some things are better left unsaid," he surmises as we walk.

His non-communicative behavior is something I would have called a deal-breaker in the past, said thank you but no thank you; I need to know you deeply; hear your struggles, know your gifts; feel your wisdom; but he's having none of that and never will; I can sense it all now; realize he's a closed bank vault, a pile of buried treasure; a forbidden land; a never-attainable Shangri-La.

But he's terribly beautiful, wonderfully compelling as he walks along the river, all lanky-legged and elegant like my dad, his strides long and easy; his scent reeking of power; but a tourist gets in our way, crowds Thomas on the sidewalk and he curses him, angrily confronts the innocent stranger. Oh my god what am I getting myself into.

When I appear confused, a little shocked, he says he got angry at them for me, to protect me, puts his arm around me, lectures me on the injustices of the world, how he's suing an officer who stopped him for running a stop sign that he didn't really run, maybe just a little, maybe going to court to fight it, might have to sue someone else too, must be proven right, correct, smart, morally redeemed.

I ask if he believes in karma, how everyone eventually feels the pain they've caused others, how that always circles back to each of us; and that no one here needs to be the judge. He looks at me and shakes his head, laughs. "That's sweet," he says. "But not true."

Later sitting along the river as the moon rises over the city, he asks about my life; I talk about Christopher, heartbreak and spiritual salvation at Shambhava. He listens, seems interested, says he knows Christopher, has done business with him. He blames Christopher for our love affair; tells me I was the victim of a powerful man's lies and that he'll protect me from Christopher during expo.

This is sweet, correct? I feel honored, sort of. But listening to him talk it's clear that his protectiveness comes with an edge; there are good guys and bad guys in his world and one must take a side; and if one falls to the wrong side of his tally for any reason it is unforgiveable, sue-able, the offender worthy of being sent away, beheaded, disgraced for eternity. This is frightening to listen to, but I chalk it up to youth; he's so much younger than me, hasn't had the benefit of time to show him the evenness of things in the long run; the spread of tit for tat on all of our score sheets when all is said and done.

He has a deep smoldering charisma and when he puts his long arm around you, says he'll protect you, shield you from all that's bad, you suddenly believe he's right, that the world is a dangerous place and there are so many transgressions after all; and geez it's nice to have someone carry something for you, lift the heavy things, and you say yes thank you thank you I surrender, hands above your head, take me into your captivity; and you've never felt so safe, so surrounded with grace, so sought after; what else could possibly matter besides feeling this utterly safe and cared for?

Of course he doesn't like my stories of Babaji. Says he once "fell under the spell of a guru" and it didn't end well. Says he's a Taoist now. "Does that mean you believe in nothing?" I ask. "Maybe," he answers.

He tells me about backpacking around the world by himself at 17, going to India to bathe in the Ganges; a mystical experience, he says; but there's more beneath the story that he's not telling; he hints of a teacher who disappointed him or worse. He won't really say.

He's clever and funny; entertains me with hilarious accounts from his day-to-day adventures supervising the production line of a large herbal tea company. We lean against each other laughing as we ride the taxi back across the moonlit river. "I've never seen such an enormous full moon, have you?" I say, bending over the boat rail to glimpse its reflection in the swirling currents; wondering if this full moon in Pisces is opening me up a bit too much, leaving me raw and exposed just when my intention was to hold it all together, to keep my cards close.

I know I'm in trouble before the water taxi docks at shore, before he walks me to my hotel room, kisses me sweetly in the hallway; then leaning against my door, takes my hand and kisses it softly, says; "Good night, I have an early morning meeting, see you tomorrow."

My hormones have come undone. I'm on fire with desire and praying to Nityananda to save me as I fall into bed alone. This damn Pisces moon.

Nothing is easy with me. I'm scarred, damaged. I flirt and retreat, quiver when he runs his finger along my arm outside a meeting, cling to him madly at a dance party, refuse to see him later when it all feels suddenly wrong; he's too young, a bit too angry, and I can't imagine what the heck I'm doing.

But we continue; courting and sparking between meetings and seminars. He charms and delights over late-night dinners, brings me a single rose each evening; but after kissing in the hallway I always retreat to my room for the Guru Gita, fighting my body's desire, watching the enormous moon slip behind tall buildings, reflect itself eerily in the currents of a dark river.

I've truly never seen such a moon; it's larger than a Long Beach moon, more golden than the moons of Shambhava; there's something illusively magical about it, can't put my finger on it, like a raven arriving to tell me a story; like suddenly knowing your life is about to change for the lovely and impossible, for the strange and disturbing, for the best of the best and the worst of the worst; and there's really not a darn thing you can do about it; somehow I know this just by looking at this moon.

Each morning I rise at dawn to chant the Guru Gita, dress in my favorite flowing rayon dresses with long matching jackets, lace up my pink running shoes to get where I'm going, pack my dressy flats for later; ground myself in the comfortable expo routine, in my happy role as executive editor, moderating seminars; assisting herbalists with the herb walk at the Baltimore botanical gardens. Thomas meets me outside the door after each seminar, a sprig of rosemary or lavender in his hand and a quick hug before we're off to our separate events. My clothes begin to smell like him and I like it. No, I love it. Truly, madly, deeply love it; keep smelling my top when no one is looking.

An audience member who I notice attending my seminars tells me that my panel discussions are the best ones at Expo because I ask the most thoughtful questions, bring out the best in each panelist. She hugs me, says she loves my editorials in the magazine. "You have a real voice," she says. "You need to write a book." I nod and thank her profusely – wondering what that means exactly and if anyone would be interested in reading my words if they were from the heart, spilling out my truth instead of prosing lightly about the benefits of herbal medicine for immunity or the life stories of amazing healers; if I didn't write about others, other things and people, what would I write? Seems like I once knew that answer.

Margaret and I spend several afternoons visiting company owners, selling ads; our work now ridiculously easy because of us, the magic of Margaret and Sue; our magazine thriving in its aura of abundance and success; our job done, our ad sold, before the meeting even begins.

"I saw you in the restaurant with Thomas last night," says Margaret between meetings. "Yeah," I answer. "Don't jump to conclusions, Margaret. He's young and immature; he's not looking for commitment. And he lives in California."

"But he's beautiful," she whispers leaning into me. "And smart. Enjoy yourself Sue. You deserve it. I'm sort of seeing someone too," she laughs.

"Seriously, tell me everything," I say as we enter a large conference room with executives waiting around the table. "Later, when we're back in Boulder," she whispers. "I'll tell you the story. Enjoy Thomas while you're here. Trust me, you need this."

But I don't know if I do. Don't know if this is just another trap, a karmic loop to break, an impossible man with no interest in settling down. Later that day, I walk alone along the riverfront, Babaji's mala in my hands, repeating mantra on each bead. Nityananda pull me out of these darn samsaras.

The next day, while hurrying down an aisle on the convention floor, I run right into Christopher. "Sue," he says startled. We stare at each other. He looks, sweet, ethereally beautiful; impossible to turn away from. "Can we talk?" he asks, his blue eyes annoying, penetrating, sexy, manipulative, sincere; just stop it, stop looking at the eyes, looking at him, don't do it, step away from the kitchen, walk away from the fire. He's happily living with his wife and family. I touch Babaji's mala around my neck.

"There's nothing to say Christopher. I can't be around you. I'm sorry." I turn and walk away quickly. The funny thing is how it hurts to see him, still, makes me want to run to him, feel his arms around me, lose myself in the angel of Christopher, the devil of Christopher, the contradictions of who and how he is, the way he's sweeter than anyone, wittier than a movie star, has a crowd parting effect on the room, on me, always seems to be just dropping in from heaven with a wonderful compliment about my looks or my writing; then spinning off, dismissing the ones who love him most, seeking his next conquest; his pattern going on and on, tangling me and others in the mess; continuing even in this minute, spinning us all down to a fine particle of dust that clogs up my tear ducts and fills my eyes with crazy salty tears.

I find a bathroom and sit in the stall crying. Calm down Sue. Let it go. Deep breath. Focus on Nityananda. I run my fingers along the mala saying mantra but Christopher's colors are all around me; until I find a raw powerful anger deep down inside, anger at the world for its inaccuracies, its illusions, false pretenses; the lovely Christmas card photos of the perfect blue-eyed family of four; when that family isn't really perfect, never is; and so many others suffer because of all it takes to keep that illusion intact, all the hidden lies that prop it up, the affairs and transgressions, that yes, I've been a party to and am now very sorry for, angry about, fed up with, and still drawn to.

Christopher thinks I'm being mean; says I'm unnecessarily shutting him out because I won't have tea with him. He makes a few more attempts to connect. Later he says nasty things to people; tells them I'm an angry, messed-up person; that he mistook sex for love. His words get back to me. I strike back like a child; tell my friends that he's a liar, a cheater and his perfect life is an illusion. I come undone; forget karma. What the heck is karma anyway? I'm the one who believes in that nonsense right? Believes that we don't need to judge each other when that's such a lusciously human thing to do; so compelling and irresistible to drop the gavel and pronounce each other guilty.

Or I'm just a loser; a wounded lover who gave my heart away and lost everything and wants to punish everyone, especially Christopher, because he doesn't suffer, nothing sticks, he's karma free, an escape artist; the Houdini of love.

But later that night while meditating, I realize that Christopher says mean things because he feels hurt, thinks I should be strong enough to hug him, dance with him at Expo parties, have secret sex in his hotel room; pretend we meant nothing, that I didn't hang my future on him. Yes, I'm angry; but for me, for now, that's a good thing and I'll try to be kinder, stop saying things, anything, about him.

That painful moment of running into Christopher pulls me more strongly towards Thomas. On the final night of Expo, Thomas comes into my room, promising nothing, filling my senses, opening my heart with his youthful sweetness, his fearless passion, his wild sex. I'm lost again, my soul floating down the muddy river; I dream of us all night; the sweetness of Thomas and Sue, walking side-by-side down a dirt road in the Pisces moon, a little girl walking between us, taking each of our hands, pulling us along.

I fly home the next day, and Thomas calls from the Denver airport, a surprise visit to see me on his way to a business meeting; we fall into each other, intoxicated with passion; hardly leave my apartment for two days.

When he's gone, I devote myself to work and to Nityananda; but something essential has shifted; I've completely surrendered to the ridiculously familiar white-picket-fence hope; the dreadful wicker-porch-furniture dream; the unbearable tow-headed-child longing. None of these things are promised or even discussed with Thomas; he dreams of dance parties, lazy afternoon hikes, surfing in the Pacific - while I am already naming our child, building our home, planning the wedding; out of control, hormone driven, unstoppable me.

Weekends at Shambhava are interrupted by Thomas's calls to the payphone in the dining hall, giggling in the corner as we talk, returning to the table red-faced and secretive. Babaji notices and calls me to the sunroom. I sit at his feet and tell him the story of Thomas. He closes his eyes, fingers moving across the mala, inhaling and circulating breath. He asks me a few questions about Thomas; studies the air above my head, communes with Nityananda.

After awhile he says: "You've brought all of your patterns to this ashram, placed them over everything you've learned, changed very little inside." But he says these words so lovingly that I sit at his feet crying, surrendering to his truth.

"What can I do to change this?"

"Meditate. Meditate. Meditate. Devote yourself to your spiritual work. Thomas may be the man you're looking for; but don't repeat your old habits with him. Wait and see what the Shakti has in store."

"Thank you Babaji. I cherish my mala from you and I'm so grateful for your offer to move in; I'm still considering it."

"I know honey, I know." He waves me off.

Driving down the canyon in a whirl of confusion, surveying my cozy apartment, my private space, the closet spilling over with brightly colored Carole Little dresses and matching shoes. I try to imagine fitting this, fitting my life, into a trunk at the end of a bunk bed in a crowded room. I try over and over to imagine it. It feels impossible.

Instead, I dream of sex with Thomas, the tall cinnamon-eyed, testosterone scented man from California who promises nothing.

The following weekend a friend and fellow Sangha member tells me she's heard about the invitation to move in and is hoping I'll do it. She shows me a room where I would bunk along with her and a few other staff members. There's no real closet, she explains sweetly showing me around, but you'll have room for a trunk and these shelves over here would be yours.

I toss and turn in my apartment, sitting up at 2 am to call on Nityananda, ask him to guide me. I'm aware that for all of Babaji's extraordinary grace, his larger than human capacity to channel in the divine, Babaji is still human - has an ego like everyone else and thus is fallible, easy to hurt - and that saying no to his extraordinary offer might wound his human heart and push his astonishing love away; the best and purest love I've ever known.

Am I willing to lose that love, that grace? For a man who promises nothing, who seems to most cherish my physical self, my human flesh, and has little interest in my soul.

I'm tortured by the way I'm drawn to the tall herbalist; so smart that his oppositions to my spiritual beliefs are thought-provoking. His questions make me wonder why I need a Babaji or a Nityananda when I have my own pipeline to the divine, as he says. No one needs a teacher, really, he explains.

He tells me that my Sangha, my spiritual community is a cult. He outlines the reasons why; there are rules and duties and the community is governed by a human being whom everyone wants

SUE FREDERICK

to please; yet he's still human no matter how stunning his presence is.

I think about this and see some truth in it; I realize that deep inside maybe Thomas does have spiritual wisdom, things for me to consider. Yet he's not offering me a future with him – says he lives one day at a time; still he flies in to visit at least once a month; we hike, cook meals, ski in Breckenridge, visit mutual friends, share an erotic love that pulls me far outside of myself, twists me up and tosses me away, lost in the rhythm of lust.

Whenever I ask what he wants from me - he says; "All I want is to die with God in my heart." I'm stunned by the answer, unexpected and correct, incomplete yet flawlessly precise.

But I don't see this divine wisdom in how he goes about his daily life; speaks to people when we're out in the world. He's often rude to strangers, sometimes to my friends; he complains endlessly about the injustices of life, of his past and present; is ever eager to file lawsuits, take more people to court – anyone really - inconsiderate drivers, malingering business associates, flawed lovers from the past. The court of law is his holy altar; his karmic temple; where he goes to worship and find redemption from a God he can't believe in.

He smells like sex; I bask in it; my clothes are heavy with his testosterone and I sniff them when he's gone; he adores my body; our sex is mind-altering. He holds me with heart-breaking sweetness, gets teary eyed whenever he sees me.

He's mean; tells me he only likes thin people; says that if I ever gain weight the gig is up; he'd even put that addendum in our marriage contract if we were considering that, but we're not. He says he'll never ever support a woman financially; that even if there are children the woman needs to be an equal partner in providing income; and that after all, he would be better than anyone at staying home to raise children, wouldn't he?

He's offended by meditation, says it's a huge waste of time when one could be doing things, doesn't like it when I burn incense; demands that I hike or bike or ski or dance each time we visit; there's no sense wasting precious time talking when we could be doing, or worse yet feeling when we could be playing, or

156

still worse talking about what we feel - when we could be hiking up Sanitas or dancing in a club.

He is ridiculously fun; we play like kids on the trails outside of Boulder and when I finally agree to go out dancing he is goofy and ridiculous; makes me laugh until I cry on the dance floor; around our mutual friends he is that charming guy, the one with unusual interesting things to say when the chatter lulls over dinner; he can be relied upon; until all at once I've offended him or someone has a tone he doesn't like, and then he's sullen, quiet, non-communicative.

He says that absolutely nothing is worth discussing ever; except sex - which is everything and very much worth discussing always. He has all the clever answers; his mind outwits me. In quiet moments he's more sensitive and intuitive than me; pretends he's not; says there's no such thing as intuition just as he calls me when I have my hand on the phone to call him.

He values the mundane with the same reverence I give the divine. He's passionate about gourmet food, fine wine, extraordinary chocolate, accumulating wealth, finding worldly success for himself. He wears only the finest clothes; folds them into his suitcase with precise creases that mimic how they looked on the shelves before he bought them; goes through my closet admiring my dresses, urging me to buy better shoes, the highest heels, the leather clutch from Coach that I can't afford. He doesn't buy me gifts except for framed photos of himself and lovely red roses.

I realize that his contradictions perfectly mirror my own struggle between the sacred and the physical; my pull to wear fine clothes, live a comfortable life, have a beautiful home; all of these desires battling my urge to move into the ashram, surrender it all, commit to the work instead of the man.

And yet I wonder - why am I here on earth if not to taste it, love it passionately, immerse myself in it fully? What's the purpose of a human body if not to enjoy its abundant sensual pleasures? In the past I've lost myself in all things mundane, in men, and it led me down a path of heartbreak. Would things be different now? Now that I'm able, with meditation and daily practice, to walk in both worlds at once; now that I'm more aware of the divine than ever before; would that make a difference in how things go?

Shouldn't I be able to keep my heart wide open to God and fully embrace this earthly world – be in it fully and not of it? Isn't this the ultimate gift that Babaji has given me? Or does my soul need to make a choice. Which way will I go? Is one way forward and the other backwards? I'm not sure.

Days later, at an evening satsang at Shambhava, I ask Babaji just that: "Shouldn't our great spiritual work here, with you, make it possible for us to live in the mundane world, the everyday world, and not get lost, not lose our connection?"

He stares above our heads, having communion with Nityananda, then says:

"Yes, when you're strong enough, grounded in daily practice, you can do anything, live anywhere;" then another long pause while we all wait; listening to his deep breathing, the room stilling; then he opens his eyes and looks directly at me:

"You have many samsaras, old karmic patterns; the question is are you strong enough to break them, rise above them? Only you know the answer," then sweetening, laughing; "Life ain't easy for a girl named Sue."

"I love men too much; love them as if they're God instead of men; and that's what messes me up, again and again."

"Of course you do, honey; many women do that," he looks out over our heads, then across the room at our faces, the women here outnumbering the men, "Most of you do that; just meditate, transfer that love to Nityananda; you'll all be fine."

I study Babaji's face; the way it's lit up from within, giggly with happiness, blissful in his connection to Nityananda; an enormous conduit of love; his lifetime of daily practice and inner discipline opening him fully to the other side; allowing his unconditional otherworldly love to pour through him and spread across this room; swirl above us and through us; create something greater than we can grasp hold of. And in this moment, this instance, of watching his boundless happiness, I know that he knows I won't move in, has known it since he first asked me to, no, long before he first asked me to; but he wanted to put a choice in front of me, something for me to grapple with; to make a decision for my higher self either way; and that both answers are right, have always been right; and the genius of this generous loving Santa Claus of a man sitting right here in front of us is that he always loves us anyway, no matter what we lay at his feet; no matter what life hands him; he transforms it into gold, into a gift; and what a thing is that; just what a kind of thing is that to offer; a precious nectar to drink from when so much of this world is wrung dry and thirsting.

I surrender to this and that; to this world and to the other; to this enormous intangible love here in this room and to the kind you can feel on your skin, against your face, in your bones when someone touches you; I surrender to the happiness of longing.

13

The Choice

Fall of 1992 – Boulder Colorado

Margaret meets me to climb Bear peak, just west of Boulder. It's the toughest climb we can do close to home. We grunt and pant our way to the top where the trees open up, the sky is bright and empty, the air freezing cold; and the wind roars like Everest, like a dragon, like a locomotive; we are so proud of our freezing selves to have made it to the top, posing for pictures and sharing water, our lips blue as the sky; but there's no better view than here, nothing like this, so we'll take it in, breathe deep, survey the distant summits bathed in wispy snow; we are pummeled by everything outside and in. "Let's get off of here before I die," I say.

We scramble down the scree, legs purple, teeth chattering, until we're nooked cozy and wind-safe beneath an overhanging rock, surrounded by tall bending trees, crazy beautiful horrible lovely lonely Boulder spread out before us.

"So tell me, Margaret, what's his name?" I ask gulping water, stomping my feet to get the blood to flow, swinging my arms in large arcs to warm my hands.

160

"It's Matthew. But Sue, I just don't know. I'm not supposed to grow attached to my partners. We've been sneaking off to spend time together and wow I'm in trouble here." She opens a bag of cashews and we pass them back and forth. I dig around in my pack and pull out my largest wool hat, my ugly hat, I call it; the one I only wear when no one is looking.

"You look adorable," laughs Margaret, "Like a Sherpa."

"It's this or immediate death. You'll just have to grin and bear it; glad I can make you laugh, but you're changing the subject. Ignore the hat. Tell me more," I giggle, handing her the cashews. "So he's part of your community? Was he assigned to you by your teacher?"

"In the beginning he was. Now our teacher is watching us to see how we'll handle our attraction. It's sort of a test. There's such a strong pull between Matthew and me. We run together nearly everyday." She sniffles. "He's so sweet, such a good man."

"Oh baby. Isn't that a good thing? To feel so connected?"

"We'd have to leave the community to be together. And right now the community is everything – for both of us. We're our teacher's favorite students. Matthew has lived with them for more than ten years. And, well, I'm sort of involved with my teacher too, but not in love with him." She looks away, then giggles, looks back at me, "It's the wildest thing I've ever done. But it's been great for me."

"Oh, this is so familiar Margaret. I understand completely. You're torn between two parts of yourself, which way to go, which way is forward? I'm struggling with a similar dilemma. Do you love Matthew? Would he commit to you, just you?"

"I'm not sure what I want," she whispers, "And I'm not sure what Matthew wants. But our teacher will probably kick us out of the community if he finds out we're in love, committed to each other. Matthew's been in the community for so long, Sue. He may not be able to function outside of it. He's a carpenter for God's sake; a gifted one; but hardly makes any money. That would be all on me. And if I want a child, well, I don't know."

"Thomas says flat out he'll never support a woman even if he's married to her and they have kids." We stare at each other wide-eyed, then burst out laughing.

"Oh my God Sue, just Oh my God," she says.

"I know! Margaret, I know! What is it with us and men? I've been thinking about this so much; Thomas promises nothing and seems to only appreciate my physical self, my body. Yet I'm completely stuck on him, like super glue, he has to pry my fingers away as he's leaving. I'm a horrendous person and unsalvageable. Please leave me here to freeze to death in my ugly hat."

"They'd put your picture in the paper, you know, wearing that ugly hat; there'd be nothing I could do to stop them," she says giggling, pointing to the hat, then falling over laughing.

"You could write my obit. What would you say?"

She pauses for a moment to think, then: "Here lies Sue, the woman who loved too much, who dreamed too much;" she looks off into the distance then back at me; "But I loved her - like crazy - until she put on the ugly hat. Then I had to kill her."

We lean back against the rock laughing; "I love that, I need to die right this moment so you can write it."

Margaret sits up straight to look at me: "Sue; you and Thomas; me and Matthew; is it what we want or not? Do they really see us? Matthew doesn't even know me out in the world, as a business woman or as anyone other than a spiritual seeker in our community."

"It's the opposite for me. Thomas only knows me, loves me, out in the world; he won't even acknowledge my spiritual life."

We share more nuts and water, study the vast colorful spread of Boulder in front of us. After awhile I say: "But I see him. I see all of Thomas, his wounds, his gifts, his struggles. I'm sure you see all of that in Matthew too."

"Of course I do. It's what women do, right?"

"We understand their complications and somehow, usually, we're able to love all those jumbled pieces. In fact we love them for those wounds."

She nods, "Absolutely."

"That's why our relationships are so screwed up," I laugh.

"But we're women!" Margaret's shoulders are back, chin tilted; "We're used to putting the pieces together for everyone; like for my complicated father, my wounded mother, your parents. We try to accept them for their contradictions, even for the pain they've caused. We love them anyway."

"It's like being a mom and seeing the great potential in your screaming toddler when no one else can see it. It's part of our DNA to love unconditionally."

We face each other now, knees touching: "Margaret I think I look at these men as children who need healing and I give them too much love; they can't return it. It's a mother's love. It's too much."

"Yes, yes, that's exactly what I do," she says, nodding her head.

"Is it just because we need to have kids, need to have them now before it's too late; is that the thing we're really wanting?"

"Sue do you remember what the herbalist said in your seminar at expo; that each month when women have their periods, their bodies are grieving a lost child. Remember how that felt so true?"

"Yes, and when a man breaks up with me or doesn't want to be with me, I feel bereft like I'm grieving the loss of a child."

"So maybe we should just have children, raise them alone, without the men."

"I've never been able to get pregnant, Margaret, never. A doctor said once that he thought there was an issue with my tubes. He wanted to do tests but I didn't want to know, didn't want to hear the diagnosis."

"But look at you now, you're so healthy and strong," leaning back to look at me, "You're the picture of health! Except for the hat."

"My acupuncturist says I'm fertile; he says he's unblocked my chi," I laugh.

"I bet he has," says Margaret giggling. She pulls out a bag of chocolate and raisins and we dig through them greedily, fighting over the chocolate pieces.

"So we have to stop loving men as if they were our babies. Or maybe I should ask my acupuncturist to really unblock my chi," I nearly choke on the chocolate from laughing,

"Hell yeah," says Margaret – then sighing; "Well honey child, maybe this thing with Thomas will surprise you – turn out better than you think."

"And Matthew, I feel good about him for you. When you talk about him it feels right."

"Oh I know honey, I know. I want it to be right for both of us," she says as we gather our things. "Take off your ugly hat; we're going into town to find baby daddies, rich ones."

"Right; ready and willing," I say packing it away.

Thomas flies in to visit and the three of us have dinner. He and Margaret swap stories about the owners of the tea company where he works and the herbal quality standards he's writing for the industry.

I'm always impressed with his mind, how hard he works, his upright gonna-change-the-world attitude; his make-people-accountable righteousness; even though it sometimes scares me, it resonates somewhere deep inside; he's willing to dig in and work hard, accomplish things, do what he thinks is right. He's not here just to play, even though he tries to make it look that way. He's not a player; he's a soldier in the trenches and, like it or not, so am I.

After dessert, she gently confronts him about not meeting my Babaji. "Thomas would you ever move to Boulder?"

"Maybe. Don't know the future. Does anyone?" he smiles playfully, illusive as always.

"Have you met Babaji yet?" she asks. "No," he says. "I'm not comfortable in spiritual groups like that. Had a bad experience once."

"Tell us what happened to you, Thomas. Was it while you were in India?" I ask leaning towards him, taking his hand, hoping he'll talk.

"It's best to keep some things in the past."

"You always say that."

"It's always true."

"But if we're in love, as we say we are, shouldn't we know the stories that make us who we are?"

"Not really," he says. "My childhood didn't make me who I am. Yours didn't make you who you are."

"But this spiritual work has been wonderful for Sue," says Margaret. "Seems like you'd want to see the retreat center just to understand what she's studying."

"I've been considering it; was thinking of surprising her;" then taking my hand he says; "Should we drive up this weekend?" I'm flabbergasted, taken aback at how easily Margaret has helped this happen after months of my pushing for it.

"Come in," says Faith, lovely as ever in a long floral dress, her thick hair pulled back into a low ponytail. "You must be Thomas," she takes his hand, pulling us into their private home high in the trees of Shambhava. Inside it smells of incense and curry.

Babaji comes to greet us, his enormous smile lighting up the entryway, his deep laughter echoing in the small house. He's dressed casually in black sweat pants and a bright orange t-shirt, his hair pulled back in a ponytail under an orange baseball cap; his presence is ordinary and extraordinary.

"Thomas," he says warmly wrapping his large arms around him. "There's a Broncos game. Wanna watch it with me?"

"Sure," says Thomas, surprised and charmed, his guard completely down as Babaji leads him down the stairs into the family room.

"Let's bring them some snacks," says Faith, pulling me into their warm kitchen, pots bubbling on the stove. "I'm always cooking," she says, almost shyly. "It's something I love to do… Wow, he's handsome. And tall, really tall," she whispers once we're alone. "How's it going with you two?"

"Well, good and then not so good and then good again," I laugh. "It's a long distance relationship. Just have to wait and see how it plays out."

"These things have a way of going how they should Sue," she says looking at me kindly. "Why don't you pour the chai into those cups."

It smells like heaven to pour it, the cloves pungent and relaxing, I take a sip and groan with happiness, "Oh Faith, everything you make tastes like heaven. Even the chai."

She laughs appreciatively; "You're always so sweet Sue, so grateful. I really love that."

Between her words and the warm Chai I feel elated, welcomed; I finally relax, decide that she's right; that things with Thomas will play out as they should and however he feels about today's visit is not in my hands. I watch her gracefully moving about the kitchen, lifting lids, stirring lentils, adding curry spices to a sauté pan.

"Tell me about when you went to culinary school," I say. "Were you in your twenties?"

She laughs and nods, seems happy to talk about it; "Yes, it was when we first moved here; I studied to be a chef at the Escoffier school in Denver, learned so much, loved it really, had always felt at home in the kitchen. And when we opened our restaurant in Boulder I was the chef. It was all pretty fun at first."

"Rudi's," I say remembering the sweet little café on Pearl Street that I visited often when I first arrived in Boulder in 1977. There was always a line outside the door, people eager to feast on the fragrantly intoxicating Indian food, absorb the exotic loveliness inside, the way it always felt refreshing, uplifting to be there; and that now I understood was because of Faith and Babaji in the kitchen, pouring their love, their Shakti, into each exquisitely prepared meal.

We serve cups of warm chai and steaming bowls of curried lentils to Babaji and Thomas, all of us perched together on comfy chairs in front of the TV watching the game; I listen as Babaji deftly asks Thomas about his work, where he lives; never prying too much, just enough to understand, to feel into his energy. They laugh and cheer at the game, raising their arms in delight when the Broncos score a touchdown.

Later, when the game is over and we've said our goodbyes, Thomas and I walk the long dirt trail back to the parking lot. I

study his face. What is he feeling? Did he like them? Has he
changed his idea that it's a cult? But he says nothing.

When we're in the car heading away on the open road,
following the slow rise towards Eldora, I ask him if he liked the
visit. He says it was fine, but he's tired now, it's been a long day,
he says, but yes he had fun watching football with Babaji. He
wants to get back to Boulder to pack for his flight home.

I want to understand him; why can't he tell me things? What
goes on inside of his sullen quiet? Is it an old pain remembered? A
new idea that he's wrestling to make peace with? A demon from
his past revisiting? Is he jealous that I have that, believe in
something like Shambhava, when he doesn't? What is it that
closes this good man down so completely; shuts the door on his
heart just when I think I've found him, unlocked his mystery; he
shuts me out, drives us silently towards Boulder, unable to speak
or even engage in the smallest of talk.

On the way home, he drives too fast, hugging the tight curves,
scaring me as we sweep down the canyon. I watch the towering
rocks spin by outside the window in a whoosh; look, there's
Castle Rock where I spent my last climbing day with Paul, and
there again on The Dome, when I wore the white tank top and
white running shorts, belaying him as he scrambled up the steep
face, effortless in his blue shirt and red baseball cap, even though
he would be dead soon, within months; but on this day he was
alive and we sat at the top, happy with ourselves, pleased with
our climb, the sharp sun warming our backs; and I felt so good
about all things; sure that it would end well, that this man who sat
beside me on this hard rock was as invincible as the granite,
would live forever like the gurgling water in the creek
overflowing below us.

How loved I felt by the way we couldn't stop talking, could
never stop trying to understand the other; the way Paul dug
around in his heart for words that were hard and true, shared
everything he knew, the good and the bad, and how cherished I
felt down to my toes, just from the way he said those things or
looked at me across the sky when only a rope dangled between
us. And now he lives just across the sky, just a slip across the sky,
just a reach away; but far from here in this car where no one

speaks and there's nothing to say and it's lonelier than the day I sprinkled ashes in a high mountain lake and sat in the primroses crying; We will die right now on this twisted road because of Thomas's anger, his tight grip on the wheel, because he can't speak it, can't frame his terror in words; we will die now, a corner taken too carelessly, too ragingly, and maybe that is okay, truly okay, and I am good with that.

Except that we don't and it goes on and on until I lift out of the speeding car, rise above the canyon walls to walk through Babaji and Faith's warm home, pouring steaming chai into our cups, inhaling the rich cloves, putting away the lentils and bread, washing their dishes, sitting happy and safe between them in the room with the altar, looking up at Ganesha with his large and playful arms, his impossible elephant trunk, and see Nityananda there standing above Ganesha, floating through the rooms, listening to us chant, patting our heads with his enormous hands.

I will break up with him, end the madness, quit taking his calls; he doesn't speak when I need words and what else could matter more than that; but I haven't visited him yet, seen his place in Sebastopol, it's only fair, he says, to see where I live, I think you'll like it, want to move there after all, someday, not now, but someday.

I fly to Sebastopol for a four-day weekend; his tiny house is down a long winding drive, surrounded by tall trees; truly in the middle of an orchard just as he said it was; in the middle of nowhere; it's strange how dim the light is, the sun unable to fully penetrate through the tall heavy branches. Thomas is kind and grateful that I'm there, has stocked his kitchen with our favorite foods; we cook together, vegetarian stuffing, roasted vegetables, apple pie from the orchard, persimmons in the salad.

Yet something isn't right for me. I feel like I've landed in a college dorm. He's a dude; his rooms are piled with papers and dirty laundry; and where I expected to find an inviting bed, maybe a large mahogany four-posted sanctuary, instead I find a mattress on the floor where we sleep. If it weren't so messy this house would be a bunkhouse in the ashram, a place of sparseness and utter lack of creature comfort or design.

I realize then that he won't move to Colorado; is still young, happy to bachelor his way through a day, too young to understand a clean bathroom or need a warm and cozy bed. I have gotten myself all tied up in the wrong things; I have made a great mistake by hoping that this young and cute surfer, this tall disco dancer, this thin and handsome herbalist would buy a home with me, raise kids, walk them to school in the mornings, be willing to read the newspaper with me over coffee and scones.

We eat in a renowned restaurant in downtown San Francisco. He's made reservations at all the right places, planned the perfect evening to stroll the city sidewalks; I ruin it; have to run and puke into a street gutter, through the grating. Almost as soon as we walk out of the restaurant I am dizzy sick, heaving in front of everyone. He is embarrassed, holds back, then steps up, closes in, puts his arm around me.

But it continues, as we drive across the Golden Gate he asks if I think it was the mashed potatoes and I heave into an empty coffee cup until we reach the park at the end of the bridge and I jump out, walk in the cool evening grass, heaving while he waits in the car. As I'm relieving the contents of my stomach of everything I have ever eaten or dreamed of eating since the moment I was born, I wonder dimly if this is the same park where I once talked Chuck down from a bad trip, saved his life with a cookie. My heaves continue; loud and embarrassing. The police arrive with flashing lights. They question Thomas in the car then walk over to me. "Ma'am are you okay," asks one of them kindly.

I want to cry, run into his arms, ask him to take me away from all of this; whisk me up into a white picket fence world, forgive my trespasses, my many wrong choices, please understand, Officer, that the tall handsome guy in the car is not right, not ready for me, and that everything is wrong actually, everything.

"Just something I ate Officer," I say in my rough queasy voice. "Thank you so much for checking on me."

One of them asks if I need some water, goes to his car and brings me a cold bottle of fresh water and I look at him like he is God; but they leave, talk again briefly to Thomas; and I finish the

169

hour on the hill. When the heaving is finally done, Thomas drives us back to Sebastopol, sullen and quiet, acting like I've done this on purpose just to ruin his perfectly planned night. Things get better with us the next day, and finally, by the day after that, we're okay.

But back in Boulder I'm certain that it's over, our soul agreement terminated; yet for reasons I can't quite grasp hold of, we continue; rising up to great moments of kind sweetness, extraordinary passion, and then crashing into emptiness.

There's the friend you have, so much like a sister, whom you adore and whom you despise. She lives in the white picket fence world and all of it is perpetually perfect and always so much better than you and your pitiful life. She has no pitiful life; no pitiful self.

She marries a trust fund baby man who is elegant and smart, likeable and sexy; and she lives like a princess in the tall house on the corner with two lovely young girls. She's always generous and kind and invites you to eat lunch in her castle where she's an expert on raw foods now and un-cooks for days to prepare a feast for you: raw lasagna made of squash noodles and almond cheese with avocado soup and unbaked sesame crackers.

And it is indeed the best thing you've ever tasted, there's no doubt that it is; and you wish you lived this way and you wish your new beau was a trust fund baby and you lived here in this orderly tall house where your job was just to be. To write. To be.

But you love her. You love her for the stream of consciousness talk that she embodies; no filter between thoughts and words; between feelings and voice; and there's a certain truth that lives inside of that, funny as it is sometimes to laugh with her; there's a truth hidden deep inside the humor and you live for that – for that one moment of truth. You live for the drug of truth.

Yet there's something so disturbing, so off, in the way she pities you, wants to take care of you because you are so clearly less fortunate than her. But you realize she was raised to be this way by her Christian minister father who taught her to judge others and yet do many good things for them, help them find clothing and shelter, feed them, because they may never make it to heaven the way you have, the way you will (since you are already assured a place beside God because of your good karma); still they are worthy of your good efforts.

Which is such a disconnect from and also completely aligned with her current beliefs in a guru from India whom she's been initiated by and whose path is the only path to enlightenment (so much better than your Babaji's path and your spiritual work - although she's very glad you're doing that – have found something to pull you out of the darkness).

And yet the underbelly of the friendship is that she is the minister of light and you are not; and yet you love her. So it's your problem really that brings you to the big house on the corner to feast on her lovely organic baby carrots with homemade nut butter dip where you study her pantry shelves with their tags and names for every item all in its correct place and not even a hat or a shoe is ever out of place; her house is an altar to order.

And you wonder what kind of chaos she grew up with that she never discusses that made her this way. And geez who does this remind you of in a weird sort of way; you realize one day she is your mother except that she's funny and sweet and never ever says mean things – only just thinks them. Yet you can always hear her thoughts and she hears yours. And so you continue.

This time, this visit, after you have admired her sweet children and the orderliness of her home and the awesomeness of her lunch and her new hairstyle and her weight loss - you dig for the truth.

But she distracts you; awes and coos over your ability to run a magazine, to survive a corporate job. She has always been the secretary, the office manager; and loves the control, the power, of sitting at a front desk and arranging everyone's lives. But she's never been the producer of content or the chiropractor or the musician – all the things she believes she is or could be if she tried.

So underneath her cooing and awing you notice this lack of praise for anything you write because she is after all the writer who will write the best selling novel someday although she'll never show you a word she has written because being secretive is what keeps her in the ivory tower, the castle, above and beyond reach.

Yet one day she saves your life. So the bond and the debt grows deeper. You're eating with her years ago and laughing of course always laughing when suddenly there's no air in the room and you look outside and know you must get up and walk there to fill your lungs because certainly there is air outside; or maybe it's just the terror of not breathing that makes you claustrophobic and sends you outside to die alone in silence - until Monique stands behind you, from nowhere she appears, feeling what's going on when no one else has even noticed, and she wraps her arms around you placing her two fists over your belly and whispers in your ear; show me, show me how to do it.

She has recognized that you are dying when no one else has; and now she saves your life as you show her how to punch your stomach and food flies away and now there's air and she is holding you and hugging you and she does, she really does, love you truly, care deeply, and she senses everything, knows what lies beyond the surface although she is perfect and you are not ; you are hurricane wounded and widowed and broken hearted and over worked and she is none of those things and never will be.

So today, years later in the fine house with the perfect family and the difficult to prepare but delectable food you say: "Monique I'm in love, terribly in love with a man too young to love me back. I adore him. Want everything from him. But he's not ready. And he's wounded. Deeply wounded. And he lives in California."

"Oh you.... Oh you.... Why... I want you to have this," she gestures to her house. "Tell me tell me..."

You describe his marvelous contradictions; the numerous ways you don't fit together; and yet there's something so deep there between you, you say. "I know I'll always love him; in spite of everything. Always love him."

"What... what....deep.....yes the soul....connecting souls..."

You continue: "He is wounded yes, but so am I. His personality is flawed but so is mine; he's awkward with strangers and pushes people away but it's driven by his desire to be truthful. And strong. He's good inside; it's just his outside is damaged. And there's something inside of the damage that's worth fighting for."

She closes her eyes and dreams a bit and then says: "Yes but he's tall and good and strong isn't he; he's a provider when push comes to shove."

And you don't ask her how she knows this; you just accept it because it's true and it's how she is, and you cry though you don't even know why; and she wraps her arms around you and says: "Yes…yes…he's good, but troubled, but good."

You continue: "He's smarter than anyone and he'll never give up on anything because he wants to do the right thing even though sometimes you have to show him which is the right thing because he doesn't always see it at first. It's his father, his drunken father who hurt him so deeply and I feel his pain, know it, understand it."

"Sue…Sue," she wraps her arms tighter. "This is a good thing… yes… he's for you… say yes to this."

And you're amazed at how she gets it after all, underneath everything; she understands it more than anyone; and you don't care that she's never met him or that she knows this somehow impossibly just knows it; you want this from her, although sometimes you hate it; but today you need it and you cry and cry and something shifts inside.

And you know that you'll always love Thomas. No matter what. You always will. And it won't be easy. None of it easy. But it's a thing in front of you and you're in it and you need to be; and it's taking you to your life, to your future; and you hug Monique and you feel saved after all. Her ministry has brought you salvation.

Over time, Babaji grows distant. Maybe it's my imagination. He's given me everything and I've given him nothing in return. I throw his gifts away. But after awhile, I begin to realize that Babaji's distance has nothing to do with me; it's a shift of energy rearranging the atmosphere at Shambhava Retreat. However no one mentions this, speaks about their sudden absences from the dining hall; meals hand delivered from the kitchen to their private home; how Babaji is seldom available for Satsang in the sunroom.

On the final morning of a retreat, Faith sits on the meditation cushion at the front of the room preparing us for the day. Her hair seems richer, fuller, shinier than I remember; she sits perfectly still, wearing a long indigo dress with the burnt sienna shawl that I love falling gracefully around her shoulders. She holds her thumb and forefinger in a little circle in front of her heart chakra, eyes closed, breathing deeply. She seems transcendent to me, translucent; and in this moment completely swept up and away from us, far beyond our reach.

"Just surrender to the Shakti," she says opening her eyes and looking around the room at our faces. "The easiest and hardest part is to surrender, open up, stop thinking, wanting, planning, knowing." She closes her eyes and inhales deeply again; there's a sweetness in the room, like a nectar you can sip from if you breathe just the right way, let it take hold of you somehow instead of taking hold of it. I open up to this, muscles relaxing, breaths coming deep and long.

The door opens quietly and we're all aware without looking, by the sharpening light in the room, the twitching of the air, that Babaji is here. His hand is on my head at once, suddenly; my breath pulled up and out of me through the top of my head, sucked up to the ethers; I gasp for it, reach for it; then he's pushing into me, through my skull with his hand; a sweetness breaks over me like a wave, rushes around my eyelids, spills across my face and down my throat, washes through my belly and I'm falling over intensely aware of how he walks through us, patting and pushing Shakti until the room screams with it and now he's at the front, looking down at Faith who sits waiting, her eyes open, looking up at him, her hands resting palm up on her knees. He places both of his hands on her head and she melts down, opens up, folds over, fills up; she has no bones, her body quivers; and watching her I suddenly, absolutely know that she's pregnant, carries a child, hasn't told us, has been transformed, completely undone with a miracle, and that this will change everything.

But Faith is like me; we've discussed this before. She's in her 40s, going through early menopause, even taking hormones to help with the hot flashes; she's never been able to get pregnant. I know these things to be true from our many conversations in the kitchen, folding laundry, dusting the deities.

"Oh no, she's absolutely *not* pregnant," says my friend Charlotte who lives there as we eat lunch in the dining hall. "She's going through menopause. It's impossible."

"Right, of course." But I know this isn't true.

The next weekend, all the Sangha members pitch in to the put the finishing touches on another new temple – a shrine to Nityananda; his altar adorned with a six foot bronzed statue of him sitting cross-legged in meditation, lotus blossoms scattered around his feet; his large index finger and thumb in a perfect circle in front of his heart. I can't take my eyes away from the Murti. We plant a garden of sage and yarrow around the cabin and clear a stone-lined path to the door.

As the sun slips away we hold hands in a circle surrounding the building, chanting Om Namah Shivaya until the night breeze sends us running to the dining hall for warm chai. I know these people, trust them with my life, even though I've never been to their homes in Denver, Colorado Springs, Table Mesa; we simply meet here for this; these transcendent moments pulling us out of our smallness; and earlier as we stood around the temple when the sun was descending; when I looked over at Faith and her vivid orange sari exploded into light, I knew things; saw the curly haired child with bright blue eyes standing right beside her. And it pulled me out of my smallness.

On Sunday I decide to hike alone to the Buddha rocks. It's a long walk and it's cold outside; I think I may be lost when the granite slabs emerge finally and I make my way to the top, sitting crossed-legged where the sun warms the boulders, unable to close my eyes, waiting for the raven who never arrives.

That night in my apartment, lifting into the limbs of the Horse Chestnut, Crissie arrives on a dream, young and healthy, curly-haired and grinning; we drift out on a boat where she points to something on the horizon, just a glimmer, something in the distance that I can't quite see, right there on the water, in the waves; she wants me to see it, it's something that I really need; but I can't see it, Crissie, what is it, tell me, just tell me; and when I look at her she's fading, disappearing into wavy lines of light.

14

THE WATER OAKS

Early winter 1993

It was always a secret favorite thing to do; to wake early and slip outside into the salty morning air, walk barefoot along the dewy grass across the lawn and up to the Water Oak. We had built a little ladder, Russell and I; just a few steps to get us off the ground high enough to reach our arms up and around the lowest hanging branch, then heave ourselves into the hidden basin, the hollowed out sacred place in the middle of the trunk, right where the branches began their journey, pulling apart and reaching up towards the sky; winding their arms high above our heads to shake their leaves at heaven.

I would nestle deep into that hollowed basin, sniffing the tree bark, inhaling it with the deepest breath I could take; it was the smell of the Water Oak that I craved everyday; it was the scent of sand and oyster shells, of fireworks and sugar cane; and it smelled the way my daddy's voice sounded when we were swimming in the shallows and he was teaching me to reach my arms deep into the wave, stretch out with each long stroke to glide across the water like he did. It smelled exactly like that.

And it was that smell that I craved most after Long Beach was gone; when we made brief visits and I would walk over to the tree, lean into it; its hollowed branches no longer able to lift me up, support my weight; but it always offered up its scent, the comfort of its magic after everything was gone.

Long Beach was my home; my only home. It didn't matter that I never really lived there, was only allowed to visit; didn't get to spend entire summers the way Russell and Davis did.

What mattered was that whenever I leaned into the tree, or lifted a shell from the driveway, I came back to me; came back to my dad.

There had been a time when I was angry at dad for not leaving mom when he was so unhappy but still young enough to begin again, to live on the water, to have his simple life. But I'd later forgiven him, realizing my dad could never hurt anyone, never break any of our hearts; because in his essence he was the holy man, the priest he never became; in his heart he was the healer, not a selfish successful or powerful man in the world who lived greedily and blamefully. He was never that, never capable of it.

Instead, he was the shepherd; he had led me deeply into Long Beach because that was his religion. It became mine.

The thing I'd taken with me, the gift from my father, when I left home in 1969, was that religion; my awareness that the voice within, the God of wisdom, the knowingness I sought would always wait for me in the scent of a water oak or the sound of a shallow wave, or the graceful arc of a seagull diving for its meal. These exquisite moments, so abundant at Long Beach, had to become part of my daily life; a way of reckoning with who I was becoming. And moving to Boulder was exactly that for me, even though I didn't realize it on the day it happened in June of 1977.

I was 26 years old, on a climbing trip with a guy who owned Columbia Missouri's only wilderness-outfitters store. He'd invited several of us from Columbia to drive out for a week of camping and climbing in Eldorado Canyon, one of Boulder's revered climbing areas. We'd all said yes, pitched in for the gas and food, packed our gear and traveled.

But because I couldn't see men as ordinary; glossed over their obvious flaws to find the hidden wisdom inside, I believed that this quiet, serious climber named Larry, this guy who owned one of our town's most popular stores, just wanted to share his favorite climbing spot with us. And he did on that first glorious day; leading us high up onto the stunning red sandstone walls of Eldorado Canyon where I found myself suddenly back in Long Beach; sniffing at the rock to inhale its earthy scent; elated at the way the wind carried a fragrance of sage from the creek-bed all the way up the Redgarden Wall to where I perched high and alone on a tiny ledge. I was home.

So later that night, when we were all sleeping in our tents, and Larry dove for me, tried to rape me, or as the guys said later, tried to choke me, really, suffocate me until they pulled him off; all of us panting and confused by the sudden turn of the night; the person we thought we knew becoming something else; I realized then I'd made a mistake; believed the story I wanted to believe; that he only wanted a friend, a climbing partner; when it was all so much more than that; he wanted so much more from me; but he couldn't speak it, say it out loud, until it was too late and his old pain of never getting what he really wanted, exploded inside, and then everything just broke wide open for both of us; sending him into a rage and me screaming and terrified into the night.

But the good part was this: that terrible night of running through the canyon; our friends pulling him off of me over and over; four strong guys struggling to hold him down while he lunged for me again and again; I'd grabbed my pack and hiked through the canyon alone when the moon had paused and I could smell the fragrant Artemisia beneath my feet as I walked, touch the mossy coolness of the rocks at the bottom of the walls to slow my heartbeat; and I felt strong; knew I was home, and that I'd find a way to stay here, create a life graced by this Long Beach, by these stunning red rocks. And I had.

And yes I had spent a couple years living wild in the mountain ranges of Colorado; all my belongings fitting into the back of my Honda Civic; spending three weeks at a time leading trips through the Collegiate Peaks, the Raggeds, the Ruby Range and along the Marble river. And that had been my religion.

But many things and people had brought me to that night of running alone through the canyon to find my way home; especially Jeff; most of all Jeff. It was the summer of 1971 after Chuck had moved on; both of us still recovering from our California van trip and from the stunning loss of Chuck's best friend Ritchie in a sudden accident; Chuck had taken off to heal his wounds, return to California and find his way. I'd stayed in Missouri, losing myself in the cooking and serving at our newly launched health food restaurant, the first of its kind in Columbia.

And one day I'd stumbled over Jeff, quite literally stumbled around him on a sidewalk while visiting friends. He was standing in the middle of the sidewalk holding on to the handlebars of his shiny red motorcycle; it was an old Indian, the motorcycle, and so was he; a young Indian - tall and lean with long pencil straight hair falling past his shoulders, parted down the middle; a thick blue head band tied around his head.

He looked like a modern-day Crazy Horse, or a reincarnated Sitting Bull. There were four or five girls, all giggly, silly, gushy, standing around him and his Indian; admiring the bike and the man. I brushed right past them to walk into the house, where it turned out Jeff lived. It was easy to walk around them, take a wide berth, because I knew I didn't want that kind of guy; a man who rode motorcycles, was more beautiful than Crazy Horse, and gathered pretty girls around him on sidewalks. I didn't want that kind of blue-eyed, long-haired beauty distracting me from figuring out my life.

I hadn't said yes the first time he asked me to go for a walk along the river; but then I did, of course; and we rode his Indian and slept in his bed and I moved into his room; and it was him who moved us into Stoneybrook Farm a month later; and that was almost as good as Long Beach with its enormous pond and acres and acres of green; and the hooting barn owls calling to us at night from the roof of our ancient, towering farm house. We lived in the front room on the corner, the one that filled with rising sun every morning through its bay window; there were seven or eight friends living at the top of the stairs and around behind the kitchen; sharing chores, planting gardens, finding our religion.

And it *had* been sweet; sweeter than anything, until five years went by and I was a Montessori teacher surrounded by innocent children all day; and Jeff was a medical technician in a lab surrounded by grown women; giggly, silly, girls who saw his blue-eyed beauty and just wanted to take it home.

He really couldn't help it; they just surrounded him; and we were young, so young then; had only been dreamers, really, until suddenly we were doers; and things settled, and he discovered women.

But the good thing here, the really good thing about all of that, was that after he'd packed up and moved in with Joy (yes her name was Joy), I'd picked up my life, reassembled into someone brave and strong; I'd signed up for an Outward Bound survival course off the coast of Maine, and it changed me, overnight. I became a fearless climber; exhilarated by adrenaline; finding Long Beach in the way granite smells; the way sandstone feels beneath your fingers; the way sleeping is always better when you're out beneath the open sky watching a moon crawl east to west, having midnight conversations with Orion; and knowing how much your dad would love this moment; just love living this way, under these stars, when the moon has become your clock and the sun wakes you every morning.

And that's the one true thing that put me inside that camping van with Larry the day he drove us all to Eldorado Canyon for my emancipation. Every moment of every day leading up to that - had really all been about finding Long Beach.

And later, when I'd met Christopher on a chairlift, he was already mine; his voice already too much like my dad's; his vowels rounded and soft, smoothed and flattened by the Mississippi River; his eyes water-blue from already being my soul mate, my Irish cousin, my twin. Or so I had thought, believing that our dads once played baseball together in the evenings, on the empty lots of Algiers, along the sprawling beaches of the gulf coast.

Christopher was essentially absolutely completely Long Beach, and anyone could see that he loved oyster shell driveways,

181

spending evenings on a porch, sitting in the gnarled branch of a
Water Oak; because he was born on the river, the same river I had
in my blood. And he understood the sound of a ferryboat whistle
and what a thing it was to sleep with the rhythm of waves.

But this was all my fault, not his; it was my mistake; believing
the story I wanted to believe; that he heard something in my voice
and recognized it; wanted me beside him always; and yet he
didn't really.

We were the grandest tragedy, the terminal disaster. It wasn't
Paul. Meeting Christopher and knowing that I knew him before I
did - even though maybe we had really done so, in another time -
it wasn't meant to be now. I'd made the mistake of remembering
him. It wasn't his fault at all.

And later, much later, on a Sunday morning at Shambhava, with
all of us gathered in the sunroom, when Babaji and Faith
announced their baby, once they were certain, convinced that it
was a child and not a hormonal imbalance; I had already known
this, because of Long Beach, and the way it taught me to know
things.

Yet when the announcement was made and everyone hugged
and cried and plans were shared to expand their home to include
a nursery, I felt altered, outside of myself, tilted, knowing
something else.

And later driving down the twisty canyon, I recognized my
own course-altering inner shifts, sharp and sudden as the hairpin
turns along the road; my car hugging the narrow bends, my body
leaning heavily back and forth, helpless in the gravity of sudden
turns.

Of course, of course, was all I could say; repeated it over and
over all the way down the canyon; parking in front of the drug
store on the corner to walk down the unfamiliar aisle where the
shelves were stacked with pregnancy tests and ovulation kits;
waiting in line to pay; proudly, stridently, placing my box on the
counter for the world to see, then handing my credit card to the

cashier and thanking her much too loudly, profusely, embarrassingly.

Feeling hopelessly disappointed when the instructions say to wait until morning, which is really so far away, a ridiculously long time to wait, when everything Crissie had told me, what she'd pointed to on the horizon, had somehow here and now arrived inside of me; in spite of everything, all of my mistakes, my mortal sins and transgressions; everything had been forgiven to allow me to have this one exquisite moment of hope.

That night as I lift into the branches of my Horse Chestnut tree, curled up inside its hollow basin; I dreamt and dreamt of flying over trees and above walls and across water until finally I flew inside a house made of light, no, just a large white house, with spacious rooms and white walls and when I flew up the long curved stairway and into an empty room, there along the wall stood a small girl, a blonde-haired brown-eyed beauty of a child wearing a white slip of a dress, leaning against the wall waiting for me.

"Are you my baby?" I ask in a whisper, kneeling in front of her.

"Yes," she says clearly; her voice sweet and resonant, familiar and friendly.

"And you're a girl?"

"Yes," she smiles, her eyes deep and clear, her face pale and translucent.

"What's your name?"

"Something soft, like Sarah." Her voice lifts and lilts into the air, floating, haunting; it's lovely and sweet, old and familiar.

"I want you to know I really *really* love you," I whisper.

"And I really *really* love you," she says pointing at me, dropping her childhood demeanor, becoming something else, something ageless and wise.

Shakti is nothing compared to this; the way this dream rushes through me, jolts me upright; heart pounding, staring up at the tree, turning on the lamp; Sarah come back to me, I love you so; tell me everything.

There was an old tire swing that Grandpa had hung from a branch of our water oak at the top of the yard. He'd hung it there with thick rough rope, the kind he used to tie a skiff to its anchor, or toss over a piling to secure his ferryboat to the Algiers dock.

I'd learned to hold on tight, wrap my arms firmly around the rope, even though it was scratchy and weathered, gnarly as the tree trunk; I'd sit on top of that tire, hugging the coarse rope, and dad would push me higher and higher until I was truly flying, as high as the tallest branches in the oak tree, soaring effortlessly, breezily, above our yard and its white shell driveway and my cousin Russell waiting below on the bench eager for his turn; and I'd swing high above my dad laughing as he pushed me, laughing while I giggled; and high enough to see Aunt BeeDee sewing new curtains with little sailboats printed on them for the boys room and Uncle Warren settling in to watch a baseball game with Grandpa in his living room, and my brothers and Davis playing pick-up-sticks near the TV while Grandma cooked her magic gumbo in the kitchen; I would soar above all of it, flying free, knowing that this was the thing; this lovely moment was everything; that the way my daddy loved me was all I would ever need to get far above everything that mattered, above everything that wounded; just a push of love and I could fly.

I would give this to Sarah; she would be loved extraordinarily; the push I'd give her would be enough to send her soaring above anything that wounded, above anything not good enough. She would have Long Beach. I would give her that.

In the morning I pee on the stick and watch its colors change from baron to fertile, from single to childbearing; from widowed to motherhood. And sitting on the bed looking up at Nityananda, I know something else.

I know that Thomas will love her; will carve wooden necklaces just for her and they'll hand-paint them in the afternoons on the picnic table in the back yard under the maple tree; and he'll create a stuffed animal from scratch; build a pattern from nothing, mold and shape the furry fabric, and stuff and sew it - until it becomes an enormous and wonderful Thomas O'Malley - the kitty she loves beyond everything - the kitty from her favorite movie that they watch after school.

And I know that someday after he's taught her to ride a bike, has attended all of her plays and recitals; that he'll love her better than he's ever loved anyone; and she will feel it when he pushes her on the tire swing and sends her soaring above the Maple tree.

And I know he'll quit his wonderful job and move to Boulder for us; give up everything to be with us; and we'll buy a sweet home where he'll teach Sarah to make tacos and friends will arrive for dinner; and it will be his idea to take her to Long Beach on her first summer to dip her feet into the warm water for a baptism - and that no matter how different we are - no matter whether we make it - he will love me for how hard I try to get it right and I will love him for the same.

And maybe those two half-perfect parts of our selves will be enough to save her.

I call in sick to work; ask Margaret to come over, to sneak away from the office as soon as she can. Then I call Thomas, explaining things briefly, saying he doesn't have to decide right now if he's ready or even tomorrow, that I'll be here, happy and okay, getting ready for Sarah.

Margaret arrives, looking a bit concerned and a bit annoyed to be pulled away from meetings. I hold up the pregnancy stick. She gasps, her hands rising to her mouth, shock registering in her eyes; then a sudden realization and tears, "Oh Sue Oh Sue Oh Sue." We fall into bed, laughing and crying, holding each other close.

Later, "Margaret, how will I do this?"

"Shh, we don't need to know all these answers today," she whispers, putting her hand gently on my stomach, looking as happy as I do; then sitting up to take care of me, "We have to feed you, c'mon, get your purse. You need a good hot breakfast."

Later after a short walk to the nearby café for scrambled eggs and hash browns, we stroll arm-in-arm back home to my apartment and lay cuddled on the bed, looking out the window at the enormous Horse Chestnut.

"That's a lovely tree," she says.

"I know. I know. It's my dreaming tree."

"I'm just a bit envious of you," she says playfully. "But things are going well with Matthew. We've been talking about getting our own place together."

She looks over at me, "I think Thomas will say yes. He'll move here. He'll step up. He's grown a lot."

"We can't tell anyone just yet. I need to see my doctor, be sure everything's okay."

"I know it is honey. I just know it," she says. "You can do this alone, Sue, if Thomas doesn't move here. Or you can do it with him. Either way you have to trust that this works out."

I call David, the acupuncturist. "You've done it now," he says laughing on the phone. When I tell him I hope it's a healthy pregnancy, not just something gone wrong in my tubes, he hushes me.

"This is real, Sue. This is happening. You're healthy and strong. Go see my friend Christine today; she's the best gynecologist in town. I'll call her and tell her about you. She'll see you right away if she can."

"Okay, thank you David, as always."

"Sue, this is all good; meant to be. Don't be afraid; it's a gift."

Later in the doctor's office I feel like I've stepped into a private club, one I've always longed to join but never had the secret entry code; and sitting amongst the large bellied women, all of us reading Mothering or Healthy Baby magazine, my happiness and hope overwhelm me and tears stream down my face spilling across the pages of Women's Day.

The gynecologist is tall, athletic looking, gives me a blood test and examines my uterus. "It all looks very good, I don't feel anything that could be a tubal pregnancy. It looks normal. And you look like you're quite healthy and in shape for your age; that helps a lot when you're pregnant in your 40s." She reassures me, confirms that I'm pregnant with her blood test.

The next day dad calls; says he wanted to give me the dates for the family beach vacation next summer. But I know he felt something else, flew to Long Beach, felt me calling him from my dream, telling him about Sarah. But I don't say anything yet; need to give it more time, get through the first trimester; figure out what Thomas will do.

Thomas calls back, sweet and supportive; says he'd like to fly in soon to spend time with me; see my doctor, figure things out.

I call Monique. She invites me to her tall house on the corner where she feeds me gorgeous melon soup with blueberries, raw salad pizza, cashew butter and cauliflower tabbouleh. She puts her hands on my belly and talks to Sarah; tells me she'll throw the biggest baby shower ever and we'll have a ceremony; everyone will write a letter to Sarah for when she turns 16.

As she says those words I see Sarah as a teenager opening the letters filled with little gifts and love notes; and I understand how happy she'll be to know that she has always been loved. In spite of everything, in spite of her losses, she will finally see it, opening those love notes; that she was born into love.

Monique will later go to the ultrasound with me, holding my hand while I lay nervous and worrying on the table until the technician shows us the pulsing blinking ray of light on the screen that is her heart, her perfect heart. And Monique will lean into me as we clutch each other and sob so loudly, so joyfully, that the technician moves away to give us a minute.

Monique, my friend who makes me feel less than, yet somehow always give me more than; has become the minister her father always wished her to be - even though her religious icons wear turbans and saris and don't eat eggs and weave a different scripture; Monique saves my life again and again.

On Saturday I drive to Shambhava, ask for an early meeting with Babaji in the sunroom. He agrees. I take a place at his feet, jubilant and giddy. His eyes are closed as he meditates, circulates breath, then looks quietly at me.

Sunlight pours in from the window behind him creating a halo of holy light around his head, his smile is as wide as the sky. He's laughing merrily, his mala moving quickly through his fingers. "Do you have some good news for me?" he asks, which surprises me, throws me off guard. I haven't spoken to anyone at the ashram; only Margaret, Thomas, Monique and David know.

"Babaji, I'm pregnant with Thomas's child," I say leaning in close. "And I'm thrilled about it."

He smiles at me so radiantly, his face morphs into my father's face, then into Paul's face; the light so bright that I have to close my eyes; Babaji is suddenly pushing me on the tire swing at Long Beach; sitting beside me on the branch of the water oak; traveling to California on the floor of a hippie van. And I see that this love is the same, each particle of it something we share, weave in and out of our lives; tugging at, picking at, but never destroying; just looping it around and around and over and through each other - until it comes back to greet us sweetly in this moment right now, sitting here in front of my Babaji as he reaches down to touch my head and says; "I know honey. This is a great gift." And then; "Thomas will join you. Give him a little time."

He laughs and laughs now, joyously and sweetly; the light pauses as he reaches down again to pat the top of my head; this time sending a hot rush of energy burning down my spine, a splash of saffron exploding behind my eyelids; all of this is followed by an intense sense of well-being; of knowing that all is well and always has been and always will be; that awareness is like a drug splashing its way through my veins and arteries and rising up into my face to explode into choking sobs of happiness.

"Sit here and rest for awhile," I hear him say from the distance as he gets up to leave the sunroom; my ears still ringing, heart pounding; a vision of shallow waves rolling towards me; things get jumbled and distorted in my head as this vapor of happiness rises up around me.

Later when I'm able to get up, I step into the kitchen for a cup of warm chai, lean against the counter; my head is fluffy. I grab a fleece jacket and a down coat and head outside. The sun is hot and promising; burning away at the winter clouds, snow melting steadily from the rooftop, landing loudly on the wooden deck at my feet.

I need to walk – get back to the Buddha rocks, find my raven, spread out on the sloping boulders.

The walk takes longer than I think it should and at a suddenly unfamiliar fork in the trail, standing under a canopy of tall pines, I wonder if I'm lost. But I'm not lost; my center of gravity has tilted, like a ship tipping starboard into an oncoming wave because its cargo has shifted below.

I press my hands against my belly and feel her there; a vibrant, discernible life force spreading out through my organs, forcing me wide open; urging my heart to beat louder, my lungs to breathe deeper.

When I finally reach the boulders and climb to the top, it's joyful to stand alone there right on the edge, breathing deeply, knowing I won't return until she's safe in my arms alive and well; wanting nothing to jeopardize the gift; my old physical determination morphing into something new – a softness – an allowing-ness, a surrender to grace.

The air here is paper-thin; a comma between seasons, between storms. It's comforting to run my fingers along the coral mala; let Om Namah Shivaya slow my racing heart; and when it finally all calms, when the breathing slows, I lift my arms into the sky, stand on the edge of the rocks and call out to the canyon, to the vast emptiness; "Thank you!" I yell as loud as my voice will rise, as high as it will lift, as far as it will carry - bouncing it along the valley floor to follow the twists and surges of the waterway as it ripples into endless waves of sound and light that merge into the Colorado River then flood over the plains into the Mississippi to finally spill out into the Gulf of Mexico and drift along the sands of the warm shallow coast.

"Thank you!!!" I call again, letting it rise up through me, as I tiptoe soundlessly into the tool shed to surprise my grandpa and he looks up at me with his extraordinary smile, holding a railing for the new swing; then slip quietly through the bedrooms where my cousins sleep, happy and wrinkled around their comic books;

then run across the oyster shell driveway to find my dad waiting by the tire swing.

I know then that all is well; and that someday mom will run across the lawn towards me when it really matters; that she'll run across the lawn from their rental car to our new front door where Thomas and I stand together joyous and sweet, our arms tight around each other, holding our new bundle; and my mother will run, like I've never seen her run, run all the way to our door to meet Sarah.

And that will be the moment I will love her the most, love my mother for everything, for the way she runs in her heels and lovely dress across the lawn, crying as she reaches out to hold our new baby girl.

And that will mean everything; erase all that came before it; just one mother to another to another; to finally just run, run across the lawn when it really matters; when that's the only right thing to do, and when doing that will change everything.

I'll forgive her the world then; and she'll forgive me; because we'll realize that most of what we do and who we become is largely a half mistake, a half wrong; and somehow sitting in the water oak pulls us above and through it - to find what we're seeking.

And maybe love always arrives looking different from what we expected; a mother's love never given in the exact way we believe it should be – a father arriving young and unready, but someday becoming just what he needs to be, in the exact moment she dreams it.

And so it goes - our chain of flawed humanity, our march of souls; all of us expanding, exploding, stretching and reaching until someday we've climbed up into the Water Oak, raced each other all day on the warm sand, tiptoed alone and afraid back to the empty house at night to get the salt; and discovered that death changes no one; that our souls always linger - rising up stern and proud to wave from an attic window, or from behind a warehouse shelf, or sitting on the steps of a newly built temple; that long after we've left here, made our loved ones cry; we still linger in what we love – in who we love - stunned by the grand and majestic water oak that keeps standing up, again and again, rising up in spite of all the damage and mistakes; the lovely water oak still reaching up to give us shelter from the storm.

I must remember to tell Sarah these things.

AUTHOR'S NOTE

This is a mostly true memoir; not a complete work of nonfiction because my flawed memory makes that nearly impossible; time gets compressed or extended as we look back upon it; and some of the scenes here have been compressed, squeezed tight into one moment, one interaction, when they may have taken longer to unfold in real time.

My desire has been to tell the truth as purely as possible. Some names have been changed to save the innocent, prevent lawsuits, and other names have been changed because they don't want to be recognized by the general public for the great work they do.

Saying that, I especially want to acknowledge my Babaji for his tolerance of this story even with all of its flaws; he's allowed me to share these things because he knows that I love him truly and am forever grateful for everything and always will be; but be warned that I've changed some details to protect him; he doesn't want strangers showing up at his doorstep uninvited.

But for the most part things happen exactly this way, as I remember them; and there are witnesses; and this is my story and I'm sticking with it.

Sue Frederick has been a journalist and a poet and is now the author of several books. She resides in Boulder, Colorado with her husband Gene, her daughter Sarah, her son Kai and their two cats Mambo and Zahra. Sue@Brilliantwork.com

For more info visit: www.SueFrederick.com

Made in the USA
San Bernardino, CA
28 July 2017